Centaur Classics

General Editor: J. M. COHEN

LETTERS OF EDWARD FITZGERALD

Letters of
Edward FitzGerald

EDITED BY J. M. COHEN

SOUTHERN ILLINOIS UNIVERSITY PRESS
CARBONDALE · ILLINOIS

First published in 1960
by Centaur Press Ltd.
9 St. Anne's Close, Highgate West Hill
London, N.6

Published in Great Britain, 1960,
by Centaur Press, Ltd.

Published in the United States, 1960,
by Southern Illinois University Press

Library of Congress Catalog Card Number 60-9249

Printed in Great Britain by A. Wheaton & Co. Ltd.

INTRODUCTION

Edward FitzGerald, the least productive of the great Victorians, wrote the best letters of his age. Indeed, he stands with Gray, Cowper, Horace Walpole and Lamb among the supreme masters of this humble branch of literature. Into his copious correspondence with his many friends, among whom were some of the greatest writers of the day, went a wealth of comment, criticism, humour, description, speculation and wry scholarship that would have been sufficient to make him the outstanding essayist, and perhaps one of the best critics of the arts, of his time. But FitzGerald's ambitions were few, his interests were diffuse, and his creative powers were broken by the fears and despondencies of his difficult temperament. Except for his free translation of the *Rubáiyat* of Omar Khayyám, he wrote nothing that has achieved popular favour —nothing indeed that deserves it, except his *Letters*, now long out of print, of which we here present a selection. To the

Victorian public, although the friend of Tennyson, Carlyle, and many other distinguished men on both sides of the Atlantic, Edward FitzGerald was almost unknown. When the *Rubaiyat's* fame began to spread in limited circles on this side of the Atlantic, rumour had it that the translator was "a certain Reverend Edward FitzGerald, who lived somewhere in Norfolk and was fond of boating.*" If we substitute Suffolk for Norfolk, and the lay for the reverend status, this rumour was not inaccurate; FitzGerald was a great lover of boats, and the major part of his life was passed within the triangle between Woodbridge, Lowestoft and Aldeburgh. Visits to London, frequent in his youth, became with advancing years progressively rarer and rarer, and his few expeditions to more distant places were not only few but extremely brief. No sooner did he cross to Holland, or arrive in Scotland than he was seized with the desire to bolt incontinently for home.

Edward FitzGerald was recognized by his great Victorian contemporaries as an equal; in literary achievement he was not so, but in the art of friendship he was certainly a master; and this mastery is ably set forth in his letters. Fitz-Gerald's letters cover a wide field of topics and interest. "Old Fitz" was sensitive to all the

---

*Quoted by A. M. Terhune: *The Life of Edward FitzGerald*; no source given.

currents of his age: personal, social, literary, philological, artistic, musical and theatrical.

Possessing a modest income which enabled him always to live at leisure, he settled to nothing seriously except to his reading —a lifelong addiction—to the art of bachelor domesticity, with a pipe and a glass always at hand for a visiting friend, and to messing about in boats, either up the estuaries, or fishing at sea. He loved the Suffolk coast, the as yet unspoiled countryside, already, as he saw, threatened by unregulated building and the encroaching railroad; and for short spells he was happy in the theatres, concert-halls and literary society of the Capital. His explorations of stranger territory were solely intellectual. He mastered in succession Greek, Spanish and Persian literature, making his idiosyncratic translations from each, and finally securing posthumous fame with his virtual paraphrase of that Persian poem in which he found the closest statement of his own fundamental beliefs, the quatrains of Omar.

FitzGerald's letters, read together, give an account of the whole of his life. For the years of his childhood become vivid in the occasional descriptions he gives of his fox-hunting father and his handsome, clever, masterful and eccentric mother, whose features, much painted by such fashionable portraitists as Sir Thomas Lawrence, bore a surprising resemblance to those of the Duke of Wellington. Indifferent to her eight children, of whom Edward was the youngest but one, she followed a life of fashion in which they were spirited to Brighton, to a two years' residence in France, to London, and back to the White House, Bredfield, her estate near Ipswich, according to her whim. At the White House Edward was born in 1809. It was a Jacobean mansion, of some size, standing in a considerable park. But in 1818, on the death of her father, Mrs. FitzGerald inherited many other properties in England and Ireland. She was reputed the wealthiest commoner in the country. Her husband, who was also her first cousin, possessed the Anglo-Norman surname of Purcell, but on her coming into her inheritance he changed his name for hers.

Edward FitzGerald was educated at a private school of about a hundred pupils at Bury St. Edmunds, in which the Latin and Greek classics were tolerably well taught. Here he formed several friendships which were to last throughout his life. W. B. Donne, the son of a Norfolk gentleman and a descendent of the poet, James Spedding, a future civil servant and painstaking editor, and Fanny Kemble, daughter of the actor and sister of his schoolfriend J. M. Kemble, corresponded with FitzGerald throughout the years; and of the three only Spedding failed to preserve his letters. At seventeen he went into residence at Trinity College, Cambridge, where he read for an ordinary degree.

Spedding, Kemble and Donne went to Cambridge also, and here too was John Allen, later a country clergyman but in his undergraduate days much tempted by the flesh. Alfred Tennyson and his group, who were known as the Apostles, were in residence at the same time. But Edward FitzGerald was a retiring young man, and only came to know them in later years. At the end of his stay in Cambridge he became intimate, however, with W. M. Thackeray, who took his scholastic responsibilities as lightly as he. Singing, writing verses, walking, drinking, endless talking—seriously with Allen, frivolously with Thackeray—were the amusement of these Cambridge days. Fitz-Gerald left the University equipped with lifelong friends, but with no notion of a career, and no positive intentions. For a while he wandered, exploring Paris with Thackeray, visiting relatives in Ireland, and staying with Allen in Pembrokeshire. He suffered a revulsion from Christianity, with periods of despondency and ill-health. The first letter in our selection, written to Allen from a family property near Manchester tells of a partial recovery of his spirits. During the thirties the focus of FitzGerald's interest changed. He remained a practising member of the Church of England and an outspoken anti-ritualist. But the arts and society engrossed him. From 1830 to 1837 his life was centred on London. Often in attendance on his mother and sisters, he neverthe-

less preferred to live in bachelor lodgings, to keep
bachelor company, and to haunt the bookshops,
the British Museum reading room, and the art
dealers. His love of old pictures was idiosyncratic. He liked to buy some old canvas for a few
pounds, and would frequently attribute his purchase to some great painter. This did not
prevent him, however, from stripping, revarnishing,
patching or retouching it, or even from cutting it
to the oval shape which he most admired. Among
FitzGerald's London friends were several painters,
among them Samuel Laurence, from whom
he occasionally commissioned portraits of his
friends.

In 1837 FitzGerald set up an establishment in a
Suffolk cottage on the edge of a family estate.
Here at Boulge, looked after by a housekeeper, he
surrounded himself with the odd possessions he
loved, received his guests in dressing-gown and
slippers, and planted his garden. On no close
terms with his brothers and sisters, he nevertheless
delighted in their children. To the end of his life
he was a devoted uncle to his nieces.

From Boulge Cottage, FitzGerald continued to
travel about England and Ireland, visiting his
friends and relatives. He began to conceive an
aversion, however, for London. Gradually he
became absorbed in the society of Woodbridge,
and particularly in that of the Quaker poet
Bernard Barton, to whom he wrote some of the

best of his early letters. Younger men also began to share his affections. For W. K. Browne, an athletic young squire whom he had met on a visit to Allen, FitzGerald conceived an affection that was mingled with hero-worship. He became intimate also with W. B. Cowell, another young man, who was working in a family business in Ipswich, but who was finally to occupy the chair of Sanskrit at Cambridge. FitzGerald encouraged Cowell to give up business and go to Cambridge, and Cowell in his turn taught his older friend Persian and Spanish, reading with him and providing him with the scholarly knowledge necessary for his translations. Cowell moreover, had married at the age of seventeen, Elizabeth Charlesworth, who was fourteen years his senior, and with whom FitzGerald himself had been and perhaps still was in love. "You are a happy man and . . .", he wrote to Cowell on hearing of their engagement. The deleted words have been interpreted as "I envy you". Fitz-Gerald fostered his passion for the bride he had lost, but remained a close friend of both husband and wife. His own eventual marriage to the daughter of his friend Barton was disastrous. It is said that the Quaker poet had on his death-bed exacted a promise from FitzGerald to marry Lucy. The marriage, described by FitzGerald at the time as "a very doubtful experiment". He came to the church wearing an old slouch hat and his everyday clothes; and Lucy's demands for a life of fashion evoked no concession from a husband ineradicably wedded to bachelordom. The engagement had lasted seven years, the bride was forty-eight, the groom forty-seven, and their attempt to share a life was called off after four months. FitzGerald devoted himself with renewed intensity to his Persian studies, and in the year that followed began his work on Omar Khayyam, which was published by Bernard Quaritch in the spring of 1859 at the price of 1/-.

In January 1859 W. K. Browne was thrown from his horse while returning from hunting, to lie for two months hideously crushed before dying at the end of March. Barton and other older friends had died while FitzGerald was in his forties. But now the loss of a man so much younger and more vigorous than he afflicted him with a horror of mortality. " All the Country round " he wrote to Mrs. Cowell in 1860, " is become a Cemetery to me: so many I loved there dead" Although only fifty-one, he began to think of his own death, and to be preoccupied with the health and expectation of life of his friends. He paid increasing attention to his correspondence, writing regular letters even to those who seldom replied. Alfred Tennyson, for example, merely instructed his wife to send FitzGerald a formal answer, though on the one occasion when the two men met over a pipe and a glass, the friendship proved miraculously to have survived. Of the ageing Carlyle, FitzGerald gathered news from his niece.

As old correspondents died, disappeared or fell silent, FitzGerald opened new relations with friends on the other side of the Atlantic, with Lowell, C. E. Norton, and other Americans who had become interested in his translations, and with Fanny Kemble, a childhood friend to whom he wrote almost every month from 1871 until his death in 1883.

In the sixties FitzGerald owned a succession of boats in which he sailed with a small crew up the Suffolk estuaries and along the coast, on one occasion, described in a letter to George Crabbe, the grandson of the poet, crossing to Holland. For a while too he was partner in a herring fishery with "Posh" Fletcher, a Lowestoft fisherman for whom he conceived an admiration amounting to hero-worship that was far more extreme than his former affection for Browne. Fletcher, however, proved an unsatisfactory partner, and resented his wealthy backer's anxious interferences. When sailing, FitzGerald habitually sat on deck reading. Once he is said to have fallen into Lowestoft harbour, but on being pulled aboard merely to have resumed his book. As he grew older, however, his eyes began to fail him, and he availed himself of a succession of paid readers, whose errors and peculiarities are often recorded in the letters. With increasing age his literary works became stranger. He became addicted to scissors and paste, cutting and reshaping his favourite books as once he had cut and reshaped his favourite pictures. He reduced Richardson's *Clarissa Harlowe* to a third its length, anthologized his favourite George Crabbe, the poet of Aldeburgh, but failed to get his selection published, and made a compendious list of characters mentioned in Madame de Sévigné's letters. But his own letters, though increasingly reminiscent of the good times that were gone, were never for a paragraph less lucid, nor was the welcome he extended in his cottage at Woodbridge or his lodgings at Lowestoft or Aldeburgh to any passing friend a whit less cordial. But visitors had to announce themselves in advance. The outstanding events of his old age were a hasty visit to the home and grave of his old hero Walter Scott, in 1874, and the arrival in Aldeburgh in September, 1876, of Alfred Tennyson and his son Hallam. FitzGerald died on June 14, 1883 at the age of seventy-four, just as his work was beginning to obtain the respect of Rossetti and fellow Pre-Raphaelites, whose writing he himself disliked almost as much as he did that of Robert Browning. Tennyson he admired, though chiefly for his early work; most of his later books seemed to FitzGerald hardly worthy of publication.

The present selection of letters has been made with a view to presenting his best passages of writing. In addition, however, an endeavour has been made to collect some of his most interesting judgments on men, books, painting and music, and to show him in as many characteristic attitudes as possible. Letters whole or in part have been taken from the four volumes edited by W. Aldis Wright: the two volume *Letters* of 1894, *Letters of Edward FitzGerald to Fanny Kemble* of 1895, and *More Letters* of 1901, all of which have been long out of print. Many more letters exist in manuscript, but to judge from such excerpts as I have seen, contain little that was not represented in the Aldis Wright collections. It was FitzGerald's habit to describe the same event in letters to various friends with little change of language. However a complete edition of his Letters in several volumes is promised by his biographer A. M. Terhune, on whose biography I have drawn for this introduction.

J. M. C.
London, January, 1960

PUBLISHERS NOTE

Owing to the exigencies of the method of reproduction employed in the printing of this book it has not been possible to include headings to letters written to Fanny Kemble.

LIST OF CORRESPONDENTS

JOHN ALLEN, the son of a Pembrokeshire clergyman. He came up to Trinity in 1828, and was a close friend of FitzGerald's at Cambridge. Himself entered the Church, became vicar of Prees, near Shrewsbury, and Archdeacon of Salop.

MARY (Mrs. CHARLES) ALLEN, sister-in-law of the above.

BERNARD BARTON, the Quaker poet, was a clerk in a Woodbridge bank, and some twenty-years older than FitzGerald. He had corresponded with Lamb and Byron, and published six volumes of verse, which was facile but not highly polished. One of the "Woodbridge wits", he was a close friend of FitzGerald's from 1843 till his death in 1849. FitzGerald wrote a *Memoir of Bernard Barton* as an introduction to a section of his poems, and married his daughter Lucy in 1856, with disastrous results.

ANNA BIDDELL, sister of Herman Biddell (q.v.)

HERMAN BIDDELL, a successful and cultured farmer in the Ipswich district, who frequently called on FitzGerald on Woodbridge market days.

THOMAS CARLYLE, the well-known essayist and historian.

E. B. COWELL, a young Ipswich maltster who had taught himself Sanskrit and several other languages, and whom FitzGerald encouraged to go to Oxford. He afterwards moved to Calcutta as Professor of English History at the Presidency College, and on his return to England was appointed Professor of Sanskrit at Cambridge. It was he who helped FitzGerald to master Persian and Spanish, and who advised him on the details of his translations.

ELIZABETH COWELL (née CHARLESWORTH) wife of the above, and fourteen years his senior. The daughter of a Suffolk clergyman, she had been a childhood friend of the FitzGerald family. Edward had once wanted to marry her, and continued to refer to her as his *Lady*. A woman of considerable intellectual powers, she wrote verses, but did not publish them until 1892.

GEORGE CRABBE, rector of Merton, Norfolk, and grandson of the poet. His father, also George Crabbe, was rector of Bredfield and a member of the "Woodbridge Wits". "Young Crabbe", some years FitzGerald's junior, although lukewarm about his grandfather's poetry, shared many of FitzGerald's other literary interests.

W. E. CROWFOOT of Beccles, an old friend and relative of the Crabbes' and a great humourist.

W. B. DONNE, son of a Norfolk gentleman, and school and University friend of FitzGerald's. He afterwards became Examiner of Plays, and Librarian of the London Library.

RICHARD MONKTON MILNES, 1st Baron Houghton, poet and man-of-letters, and the editor of Keats. He had been a member of the Cambridge *Apostles*.

CHARLES KEENE, the *Punch* artist, a frequent guest of FitzGerald's in his last years.

FANNY KEMBLE, actress and daughter of the actor manager, whose wife had been a close friend of FitzGerald's mother. She had married in America but divorced her husband. FitzGerald's correspondence with her began in 1871 and continued until his death. He made a practice of writing once a month at full moon, Fanny Kemble sometimes visited England and the Continent, and occasionally met FitzGerald in London.

SAMUEL LAURENCE, a portrait painter, whom FitzGerald met in London, and who painted most of the great Victorian men of letters. FitzGerald commissioned him to make portraits of Alfred Tennyson, Thackeray, Allen and James Spedding.

J. R. LOWELL, American poet, essayist and diplomat, who was Minister in Madrid and afterwards in London.

CHARLES MERIVALE, Dean of Ely, and a member of the Cambridge *Apostles*.

C. E. NORTON, Professor of Fine Arts at Harvard, and an early admirer of the *Rubáiyat*.

SIR W. F. POLLOCK, a contemporary of FitzGerald's at Trinity and a lifelong friend. He had a successful career at the Bar, though all the time keeping up his literary connections, and was finally made Queen's Remembrancer.

FREDERICK TENNYSON, elder brother of the Laureate, and himself a poet. Married an Italian and lived much of his life in Italy. He was an Anglo-Israelite and a Spiritualist. FitzGerald admired some of his poems, and was anxious to publish a selection.

ANNE THACKERAY RITCHIE, daughter of W. M. Thackeray and author of *Memoirs*. FitzGerald left her £500 in his will.

W. H. THOMPSON, a member of the Cambridge *Apostles*, and afterwards Master of Trinity.

R. C. TRENCH, another of the Cambridge *Apostles*. He became Dean of Westminster, and, like Fitz-Gerald, made some translations of Calderón, he was later made Archbishop of Dublin.

THOMAS WOOLNER, well-known Victorian sculptor.

W. ALDIS WRIGHT, Bursar of Trinity and editor of FitzGerald's *Letters and Remains*, a close friend of his later years.

LETTERS

OF

EDWARD FITZGERALD

To John Allen.

[CASTLE IRWELL]
MANCHESTER, *February 24*, 1833.

DEAR ALLEN,

. . . I am fearful to boast, lest I should lose what I boast of: but I think I have achieved a victory over my evil spirits here: for they have full opportunity to come, and I often observe their approaches, but hitherto I have managed to keep them off. Lord Bacon's Essay on Friendship is wonderful for its truth: and I often feel its truth. He says that with a Friend 'a man *tosseth* his thoughts,' an admirable saying, which one can understand, but not express otherwise. But I feel that, being alone, one's thoughts and feelings, from want of communication, become heaped up and clotted together, as it were: and so lie like undigested food heavy upon the mind: but with a friend one *tosseth* them about, so that the air gets between them, and keeps them fresh and sweet. I know not from what metaphor Bacon took his 'tosseth,' but it seems to me as if it was from the way haymakers toss hay, so that it does not press into a heavy lump, but is tossed about in the air, and separated, and thus kept sweet. . . .

Your most affectionate friend,

E. FITZGERALD.

1

To W. B. Donne.[1]

GELDESTONE, *Sept.* 27, [1833].

DEAR DONNE,

. . . As to my history since I have seen you, there is little to tell. `Divinity is not outraged by your not addressing me as a Reverend—I not being one. I am a very lazy fellow, who do nothing: and this I have been doing in different places ever since I saw you last. I have not been well for the last week: for I am at present rather liable to be overset by any weariness (and where can any be found that can match the effect of two Oratorios?), since for the last three months I have lived on vegetables—that is, I have given up meat. When I was talking of this to Vipan, he told me that you had once tried it, and given it up. I shall hear your account of its effect on you. The truth is, that mine is the wrong time of life to begin a change of that kind: it is either too early, or too late. But I have no doubt at all of the advantage of giving up meat: I find already much good from it, in lightness and airiness of head, whereas I was always before clouded and more or less morbid

---

[1] 'My dear Donne,'. as FitzGerald called him, 'who shares with Spedding my oldest and deepest love.' He afterwards succeeded J. M. Kemble as Licenser of Plays. The late Master of Trinity, then Greek Professor, wrote to me of him more than five and twenty years ago, 'It may do no harm that you should be known to Mr. Donne, whose acquaintance I hope you will keep up. He is one of the finest gentlemen I know, and no ordinary scholar—remarkable also for his fidelity to his friends.'

after meat. The loss of strength is to be expected: I shall keep on and see if that also will turn, and change into strength. I have almost Utopian notions about *vegetable diet*, begging pardon for making use of such a vile, Cheltenhamic, phrase. Why do you not bring up your children to it? To be sure, the chances are, that, after guarding their vegetable morals for years, they would be seduced by some roast partridge with bread sauce, and become ungodly. This actually happened to the son of a Dr. Newton who wrote a book [1] about it and bred up his children to it—but all such things I will tell you when I meet you. Gods! it is a pleasant notion that one is about to meet an old acquaintance in a day or two.

Believe me then your most sincere friend,

E. FitzGerald.

Pipes—are their names ever heard with you? I have given them up, except at Cambridge. But the word has something sweet in it — Do you ever smoke?

7 Southampton Row, Bloomsbury,
[*Oct.* 25, 1833.]

Dear Donne,

. . . As to myself, and my diet, about which you give such excellent advice: I am still determined to

---

[1] The Return to Nature, or, a Defence of the Vegetable Regimen, dedicated to Dr. W. Lambe, and written in 1811. It was printed in 1821 in The Pamphleteer, No. 38, p. 497.

give the diet I have proposed a good trial : a year's trial. I agree with you about vegetables, and soups : but my diet is chiefly *bread*: which is only a little less nourishing than flesh : and, being compact, and baked, and dry, has none of the washy, diluent effects of green vegetables. I scarcely ever touch the latter : but only pears, apples, etc. I have found no benefit yet ; except, as I think, in more lightness of spirits : which is a great good. But I shall see in time.

I am living in London in the quarter of the town which I have noticed above : in a very happy bachelor-like way. Would you would come up here for a few days. I can give you bed, board, etc. Do have some business in town, please. Spedding is here : taking lessons of drawing, before he goes for good into Cumberland : whither, for my sake and that of all his friends, I wish he never would go : for there are few such men, as far [as] I know. He and I have been theatricalizing lately. We saw an awful Hamlet the other night—a Mr. Serle—and a very good Wolsey, in Macready : and a very bad Queen Catherine, in Mrs. Sloman, whom you must re-member. I am going to-night to see Macready in Macbeth : I have seen him before in it : and I go for the sake of his two last acts, which are amazingly fine, I think. . . . I am close to the British Museum, in which I take great pleasure in reading in my rambling way. I hear of Kemble lately that he has been mak-ing some discoveries in Anglo-Saxon MSS. at Cam-bridge that, they say, are important to the interests of the church : and there is talk of publishing them, I believe.   He is a strange fellow for that fiery industry of his : and, I am sure, deserves some steady recompense.

Tennyson has been in town for some time : he has been making fresh poems, which are finer, they say, than any he has done.   But I believe he is chiefly meditating on the purging and subliming of what he has already done : and repents that he has published at all yet.   It is fine to see how in each succeeding poem the smaller ornaments and fancies drop away, and leave the grand ideas single. . . .

I have lately bought a little pamphlet which is very difficult to be got, called The Songs of Innocence, written and adorned with drawings by W. Blake (if you know his name) who was quite mad, but of a madness that was really the elements of great genius ill-sorted : in fact, a genius with a screw loose, as we used to say.   I shall shew you this book when I see you : to me there is particular interest in this man's writing and drawing, from the strangeness of the constitution of his mind.   He was a man that used to see visions : and make drawings and paintings of Alexander the Great, Cæsar, etc., who, he declared, stood before him while he drew. . . .

Your very affectionate friend,

E. FitzGerald.

7 SOUTHAMPTON ROW,
Nov. 19, 1833.

DEAR DONNE,

. . .Spedding
and I went to see Macready in Hamlet the other
night : with which he was pretty well content, but not
wholly. For my part, I have given up deciding on
how Hamlet should be played : or rather have decided
it shouldn't be played at all. I take pleasure in reading things I don't wholly understand ; just as the old
women like sermons : I think it is of a piece with an
admiration of all Nature around us. I think there is
a greater charm in the half meanings and glimpses of
meaning that come in through Blake's wilder visions :
though his difficulties arose from a very different
source from Shakespeare's. But somewhat too much
of this. I suspect I have found out this as an useful
solution, when I am asked the meaning of any thing
that I am admiring, and don't know it.

Believe me, dear Donne, to be ever your affectionate friend, E. FitzGERALD.

FitzGerald spent the May term of 1834 at Cambridge 'rejoicing in the sunshine ⌣ james Spedding's
presence.'

[LONDON, 17 GLOUCESTER STREET, QUEEN SQUARE].
1834.

DEAR DONNE,

. . . I have been buying two Shakespeares, a
second and third Folio—the second Folio pleases me
much : and I can read him with a greater zest now.
One had need of a big book to remember him by : for

he is lost to the theatre : I saw Mr. Vandenhoff play Macbeth in a sad way a few nights ago : and such a set of dirty ragamuffins as the rest were could not disgrace any country barn.   Manfred I have missed by some chance : and I believe 'it was all for the best' as pious people say.   The Theatre is bare beyond anything I ever saw : and one begins to hope that it has touched the bottom of its badness, and will rise again.   I was looking the other day at Sir W. Davenant's alteration of Macbeth : who dies, saying, 'Farewell, vain world : and that which is vainest in't, Ambition !'

Edgeworth, whom I think you remember at Cambridge, is come to live in town : and I see him often at the Museum.   The want of books chiefly drove him from Italy : besides that he tells me he likes a constant change of scenes and ideas, and would be always about if he could.   He is a very original man I think, and throws out much to be chewed and digested : but he is deficient in some elements that must combine to govern my love and admiration. He has much imagination of head, but none of heart : perhaps these are absurd distinctions : but I am no hand at these definitions.   His great study is metaphysics : and Kant is his idol.   He is rather without company in London, and I wish much to introduce him to such men as I know : but most of your Apostolic party who could best exchange ideas with him are not in town.   He is full of his subjects, and only wants opponents to tilt at. . . .

To John Allen.

WHERSTEAD, *July* 4, 1835.

DEAR ALLEN,

. . . My brother John's wife, always delicate, has had an attack this year, which she can never get over : and while we are all living in this house cheerfully, she lives in separate rooms, can scarcely speak to us, or see us : and bears upon her cheek the marks of death. She has shewn great Christian dignity all through her sickness : was the only cheerful person when they supposed she could not live : and is now very composed and happy. You say sometimes how like things are to dreams : or, as I think, to the shifting scenes of a play. So does this place seem to me. All our family, except my mother, are collected here : all my brothers and sisters, with their wives, husbands, and children : sitting at different occupations, or wandering about the grounds and gardens, discoursing each their separate concerns, but all united into one whole. The weather is delightful : and when I see them passing to and fro, and hear their voices, it is like scenes of a play. I came here only yesterday. I have much to tell you of : I mean, much in my small way : I will keep all till I see you, for I don't know with what to begin in a letter. . . .

Edgeworth introduced me to his wife and sister-in-law, who are very handsome Spanish ladies, seemingly of excellent sense. The wife is the gentler, and more feminine : and the sister more regularly handsome, and vivacious. I think that he is a very remarkable

8

man : and I like him more the more I see of him.

What you say of Tennyson and Wordsworth is not, I think, wholly just. I don't think that a man can turn himself so directly to the service of morality, unless naturally inclined : I think Wordsworth's is a natural bias that way. Besides, one must have labourers of different kinds in the vineyard of morality, which I certainly look up to as the chief object of our cultivation : Wordsworth is first in the craft : but Tennyson does no little by raising and filling the brain with noble images and thoughts, which, if they do not direct us to our duty, purify and cleanse us from mean and vicious objects, and so prepare and fit us for the reception of the higher philosophy. A man might forsake a drunken party to read Byron's Corsair : and Byron's Corsair for Shelley's Alastor : and the Alastor for the Dream of Fair Women or the Palace of Art : and then I won't say that he would forsake these two last for anything of Wordsworth's, but his mind would be sufficiently refined and spiritualised to admit Wordsworth, and profit by him : and he might keep all the former imaginations as so many pictures, or pieces of music, in his mind. But I think that you will see Tennyson acquire all that at present you miss : when he has *felt* life, he will not die fruitless of instruction to man as he is. But I dislike this kind of criticism, especially in a letter. I don't know any one who has thought out any thing so little as I have. I don't see to any end, and should keep silent till I have got a little more, and that little better arranged.

DEAR ALLEN,

Have you done with my Doctor? If you have, will you send him to me here: Boulge Hall, Woodbridge, per Shannon Coach? You may book it at the Boar and Castle, Oxford Street, close by Hanway Passage. This is not far out of your beat. Perhaps I should not have sent for this book (it is Bernard Barton the Quaker who asks to read it) but that it gives me an excuse also to talk a little to you. Ah! I wish you were here to walk with me now that the warm weather is come at last. Things have been delayed but to be more welcome, and to burst forth twice as thick and beautiful. This is boasting however, and counting of the chickens before they are hatched: the East winds may again plunge us back into winter: but the sunshine of this morning fills one's pores with jollity, as if one had taken laughing gas. Then my house is getting on: the books are up in the bookshelves and do my heart good: then Stothard's Canterbury Pilgrims are over the fireplace: Shakespeare in a recess: how I wish you were here for a day or two! My sister is very well and cheerful and we have kept house very pleasantly together. My brother John's wife is, I fear, declining very fast:

it is very probable that I shall have to go and see her before long: though this is a visit I should gladly be spared. They say that her mind is in a very beautiful state of peacefulness. She *may* rally in the summer: but the odds are much against her. We shall lose a perfect Lady, in the complete sense of the word, when she dies.

To Bernard Barton.

LONDON, *April,* 1838.

DEAR SIR,

John, who is going down into Suffolk, will I hope take this letter and despatch it to you properly. I write more on account of this opportunity than of anything I have to say: for I am very heavy indeed with a kind of Influenza, which has blocked up most of my senses, and put a wet blanket over my brains. This state of head has not been improved by trying to get through a new book much in fashion—Carlyle's French Revolution—written in a German style. An Englishman writes of French Revolutions in a German style. People say the book is very deep: but it appears to me that the meaning *seems* deep from lying under mystical language. There is no repose, nor equable movement in it: all cut up into short sentences half reflective, half narrative; so that one labours through it as vessels do through what is called a short sea—small, contrary going waves caused by shallows, and straits, and meeting tides, etc. I like to sail before the wind over the surface of an even-rolling eloquence, like that of Bacon or the Opium Eater. There is also pleasant fresh water sailing with such writers as Addison; is there any *pond*-sailing in literature? that is, drowsy, slow, and of small compass? Perhaps we may say, some Sermons. But this is only conjecture. Certainly Jeremy Taylor rolls along as majestically as any of them. We have had Alfred Tennyson here; very droll, and very wayward: and much sitting up of nights till two and three in the morning with pipes in our mouths: at which good hour we would get Alfred to give us some of his magic music, which he does between growling and smoking; and so to bed. All this has not cured my Influenza as you may imagine: but these hours shall be remembered long after the Influenza is forgotten.

I have bought scarce any new books or prints: and am not sorry to see that I want so little more. One large purchase I have made however, the Biographie Universelle, 53 Octavo Volumes. It contains everything, and is the very best thing of its kind, and so referred to by all historians, etc. Surely nothing is more pleasant than, when some name crosses one, to go and get acquainted with the owner of the name: and this Biographie really has found places for people whom one would have thought almost too small for so comprehensive a work—which sounds like a solecism, or Bull, does it not?

EDWARD FITZGERALD

[LONDON, 8 *June*, 1838.]

DEAR SIR,

. . .I do not know very much of Salvator : is he not rather a melodramatic painter ? No doubt, very fine in his way. But Claude and the two Poussins are the great ideal painters of Landscape. Nature looks more stedfast in them than in other painters : all is wrought up into a quietude and harmony that seem eternal. This is also one of the mysterious charms in the Holy Families of Raffaelle and of the early painters before him : the faces of the Madonnas are beyond the discomposure of passion, and their very draperies betoken an Elysian atmosphere where wind never blew. The best painter of the unideal Christ is, I think, Rembrandt : as one may see in his picture at the National Gallery, and that most wonderful one of our Saviour and the Disciples at Emmaus in the Louvre : there they sit at supper as they might have sat. Rubens and the Venetian Painters did neither one thing nor the other : their Holy figures are neither ideal nor real : and it is incongruous to see one of Rubens' brawny boors dressed up in the ideal red and blue drapery with which the early Italians clothed their figures of Christ.

To John Allen.

[28 *April*, 1839.]

MY DEAR ALLEN,

. . .Here I live with tolerable content : perhaps with as much as most people arrive at, and what if one were properly grateful one would perhaps call perfect happiness. Here is a glorious sunshiny day : all the morning I read about Nero in Tacitus lying at full length on a bench in the garden : a nightingale singing, and some red anemones eyeing the sun manfully not far off. A funny mixture all this : Nero, and the delicacy of Spring : all very human however. Then at half past one lunch on Cambridge cream cheese : then a ride over hill and dale : then spudding up some weeds from the grass : and then coming in, I sit down to write to you, my sister winding red worsted from the back of a chair, and the most delightful little girl in the world chattering incessantly. So runs the world away. You think I live in Epicurean ease : but this happens to be a jolly day : one isn't always well, or tolerably good, the weather is not always clear, nor nightingales singing, nor Tacitus full of pleasant atrocity. But such as life is, I believe I have got hold of a good end of it. . . .

HALVERSTOWN, *Sunday, Oct.* 20, [1839].

MY DEAR SIR,

I am very glad that you lifted yourself at last from your mahogany desk, and took such a trip as you describe in your last letter. I don't think you could have made a better in the same given space of time. It is some years since I have seen the Castle at Windsor, except from Eton. The view from the Terrace is the noblest I know of, taking it with all its associations together. Gray's Ode rises up into the mind as one looks around—does it not?—a sure proof that, however people may condemn certain conceits and expressions in the poem, the spirit of it is genuine. 'Ye distant spires, ye antique towers'— very large and noble, like the air that breathes upon one as one looks down along the view. My brother John told me he thought the Waterloo gallery very fine: the portraits by Sir Thomas almost as fine as Vandyke. You saw them, of course. You say nothing of having seen the National Gallery in London: indeed I rather fear it is closed these two months. This is a great loss to you: the Rubens landscape you would never have forgot. Thank you for the picture of my dear old Bredfield which you have secured for me: it is most welcome. Poor Nursey once made me a very pretty oil sketch of it: but I gave it to Mr. Jenney. By all means have it engraved for the pocket book: it is well worthy. Some of the tall ash trees about it used to be visible at sea: but I think their topmost branches are decayed now. This circumstance I put in, because it will tell in your verse illustration of the view. From the road before the lawn, people used plainly to see the topmasts of the men-of-war lying in Hollesley bay during the war. I like the idea of this: the old English house holding up its enquiring chimneys and weathercocks (there is great physiognomy in weathercocks) toward the far-off sea, and the ships upon it. How well I remember when we used all to be in the Nursery, and from the window see the hounds come across the lawn, my Father and Mr. Jenney in their hunting caps, etc., with their long whips—all Daguerreotyped into the mind's eye now—and that is all. Perhaps you are not civilised enough to know what Daguerreotype is: no more do I well. We were all going on here as merrily as possible till this day week, when my Piscator got an order from his Father to go home directly. So go he would the day after. I wanted to go also: but they would have me stay here ten days more. So I stay: I suppose I shall be in London toward the end of this week however: and then it will not be long before I pay you a visit. . . .

To W. F. Pollock.

[Postmark *May* 3, 1840.]

MY DEAR POLLOCK,

. .It must be very nearly half-past 9 I am sure: ring the bell for the tea-things to be removed—pray turn the lamp—at 10 the married people go to bed: I sit up till 12, sometimes diverging into the kitchen, where I smoke amid the fumes of cold mutton that has formed (I suppose) the maids' supper. But the pleasant thing is to wake early, throw open the window, and lie reading in bed. Morning, noon, and night we look at the barometer, and make predictions about the weather. The wheat begins to look yellow; the clover layers are beginning to blossom, before they have grown to any height; and the grass won't grow: stock, therefore, will be very cheap, because of the great want of keep. That is poetry. Have you been down to Kitlands [1] with that mad wag Spedding?

My brother-in-law is fallen fast asleep over Buckland's Bridgewater Treatise—his breathing approaches a snore. Now could I drink hot blood. I will write no more. Clarendon shall wind up the night with me.

To Frederic Tennyson.

THE CORPORATE TOWN OF BEDFORD,
June 7, 1840.

DEAR FREDERIC,

Your letter dated from the Eternal City on the 15th of May reached me here two days ago. Perhaps you have by this time left Naples to which you bid me direct: or will have left it by the time my letter gets there. . . . Our letters are dated from two very different kinds of places: but perhaps equally well suited to the genius of the two men. For I am becoming more hebete every hour: and have not even the ambition to go up to London all this spring to see the Exhibitions, etc. I live in general quietly at my brother-in-law's in Norfolk and I look with tolerable composure on vegetating there for some time to come, and in due time handing out my eldest nieces to waltz, etc., at the County Balls. People affect to talk of this kind of life as very beautiful and philosophical: but I don't: men ought to have an ambition to stir, and travel, and fill their heads and senses: but so it is. Enough of what is now generally called the subjective style of writing. This word

[1] Where D. D. Heath lived.

has made considerable progress in England during the year you have been away, so that people begin to fancy they understand what it means. I have been striving at it, because it is a very *sine qua non* condition in a book which I have just been reading, Eastlake's translation of Goethe's Theory of Colours. I recommend it to you, when you can get hold of it. Come back to England quick and read my copy. Goethe is all in opposition to Newton : and reduces the primitive colours to two. Whewell, I believe, does not patronise it : but it is certainly very Baconically put together. While you are wandering among ruins, waterfalls, and temples, and contemplating them as you sit in your lodgings, I poke about with a book and a colour-box by the side of the river Ouse—quiet scenery enough—and make horrible sketches. The best thing to me in Italy would be that you are there. But I hope you will soon come home and install yourself again in Mornington Crescent. I have just come from Leamington : while there, I met Alfred by chance : we made two or three pleasant excursions tog her : to Stratford upon Avon and Kenilworth, etc. Don't these names sound very thin amid your warm southern nomenclature ? But I'll be bound you would be pleased to exchange all your fine burnt up places for a look at a Warwickshire pasture every now and then during these hot days. . . .

The sun shines very bright, and there is a kind of bustle in these clean streets, because there is to be a grand True Blue dinner in the town Hall. Not that

I am going: in an hour or two I shall be out in the fields rambling alone. I read Burnet's History—ex pede Herculem. Well, say as you will, there is not, and never was, such a country as Old England—never were there such a Gentry as the English. They will be the distinguishing mark and glory of England in History, as the Arts were of Greece, and War of Rome. I am sure no travel would carry me to any land so beautiful, as the good sense, justice, and liberality of my good countrymen make this. And I cling the closer to it, because I feel that we are going down the hill, and shall perhaps live ourselves to talk of all this independence as a thing that has been. To none of which you assent perhaps. At all events, my paper is done, and it is time to have done with this solemn letter. I can see you sitting at a window that looks out on the bay of Naples, and Vesuvius with a faint smoke in the distance: a half-naked man under you cutting up watermelons, etc. Haven't I seen it all in Annuals, and in the Ballet of Massaniello long ago?

To Bernard Barton.

BEDFORD, *Aug.* 31/40.

DEAR SIR,

I duly received your letter. I am just returned from staying three days at a delightful Inn by the river Ouse, where we always go to fish. I dare say I have told you about it before. The Inn is the cleanest, the sweetest, the civillest, the quietest, the liveliest, and the cheapest that ever was built or conducted. Its name, the Falcon of Bletsoe. On one side it has a garden, then the meadows through which winds the Ouse : on the other, the public road, with its coaches hurrying on to London, its market people halting to drink, its farmers, horsemen, and foot travellers. So, as one's humour is, one can have whichever phase of life one pleases : quietude or bustle ; solitude or the busy hum of men : one can sit in the principal room with a tankard and a pipe and see both these phases at once through the windows that open upon either. But through all these delightful places they talk of leading railroads : a sad thing, I am sure : quite impolitic. But Mammon is blind.

To W. F. Pollock.

DEAR POLLOCK,

. I live in a house full of jolly children : and the day passes in eating, drinking, swinging, riding, driving, talking and doing nonsense : the intervals being filled with idleness. I hear a nephew of eight years old say his Latin Grammar : to-day we say the verb moneo—in this way—moneo, mones, monui, monuorum, monuarum, monuorum—then I thought it was time to stop. But it was a good shot.

When one talks in this sort of way, I am sure it must seem as if one considered oneself very sublimely philosophical, etc.—but I don't—my digestion is very good : and everybody here is very kind and well-behaved, and there never was such fine weather since the world began. Also, I have had Fielding to read, while smoking in the garden.

You see that all this is a mighty pleasant kind of life to lead, but not easy to write about. You must *therefore* (a pretty consequence) write to me : and tell Spedding to do so : and if old Alfred is in London, or at his country house, stir him up. Not that he will be stirred up. But I really do like very much to hear of my friends, and about pyroglyphs,[1] etc. I wish very much also to step into the pit of Drury Lane and to hear Fidelio once a week.

So take pity, and ask others to take pity, on a poor devil who is rather too well off : and let a London letter slide once in a while out of the Beccles post-bag.

Does the word Beccles put you in mind of hooks and eyes?

GELDESTONE HALL, BECCLES,
May 29/41.

To Bernard Barton.

EDGEWORTHSTOWN,
September 2/41.

MY DEAR BARTON,

You must allow I am a good correspondent—this

half year at least. This is Septr. 2, a most horrible day for a Bazaar, judging at least by the weather here. But you may be better off. I came to this house a week ago to visit a male friend, who duly started to England the day before I got here. I therefore found myself domiciled in a house filled with ladies of divers ages—Edgeworth's wife, aged—say 28—his mother aged 74—his sister (the great Maria) aged 72 — and another cousin or something — all these people very pleasant and kind: the house pleasant: the grounds ditto: a good library : . . . so here I am quite at home. But surely I must go to England soon : it seems to me as if that must take place soon : and so send me a letter directed to me at Mr. Watcham's, Naseby, Thornby. Those places are in England. You may put Northampton after Thornby if you like. I am going to look at the winding up of the harvest there.

I am now writing in the Library here : and the great Authoress is as busy as a bee making a catalogue of her books beside me, chattering away. We are great friends. She is as lively, active, and cheerful as if she were but twenty ; really a very entertaining person. We talk about Walter Scott whom she adores, and are merry all the day long. I have read about thirty-two sets of novels since I have been here : it has rained nearly all the time.

I long to hear how the Bazaar went off : and so I beg you to tell me all about it. When I began this letter I thought I had something to say : but I believe the truth was I had nothing to do. When you see my dear Major [1] give him my love, and tell him I wish he were here to go to Connemara with me: I have no heart to go alone. The discomfort of Irish inns requires a companion in misery. This part of the country is poorer than any I have yet seen: the people becoming more Spanish also in face and dress. Have you read The Collegians? [2]

I have now begun to sketch heads on the blotting paper on which my paper rests—a sure sign, as Miss Edgeworth tells me, that I have said quite enough. She is right. Good-bye. In so far as this country is Ireland I am glad to be here: but inasmuch as it is not England I wish I were there.

BRIGHTON, *Dec.* 29, 1841.

MY DEAR BARTON,

The account you give of my old Squire 'that he is in a poorish way' does not satisfy me: and I want you to ask Mr. Jones the surgeon, whom you know, and who used to attend on the Squire,— to ask him, I say, how that Squire is. He has been ill for the last two or three winters, and may not be worse now than before. He is one of our oldest friends: and though he and I have not very much in common, he is a part of my country of England, and involved in the very idea of the quiet fields of Suffolk.

[1] Major Moor of Great Bealings; author of The Hindu Pantheon, Suffolk Words, Oriental Fragments, etc.

[2] By Gerald Griffin.

He is the owner of old Bredfield House in which I was born—and the seeing him cross the stiles between Hasketon and Bredfield, and riding with his hounds over the lawn, is among the scenes in that novel called The Past which dwell most in my memory. What is the difference between what has been, and what never has been, *none?* At the same time this Squire, so hardy, is indignant at the idea of being ill or laid up: so one must inquire of him by some roundabout means. . . .

We had a large party here last night: Horace Smith came: like his brother James, but better looking: and said to be very agreeable. Do you [know] that he gives a dreadful account of Mrs. Southey: that meek and Christian poetess: he says, she's a devil in temper. He told my mother so: had you heard of this? I don't believe it yet: one ought not so soon, ought one?

Goodbye.

[GELDESTONE, *Jan.* 1842.]

MY DEAR SIR,

You tell my Father you mean to write a Poem about my invisibility—and somehow it seems strange to myself that I have been so long absent from Woodbridge. It was a toss up (as boys say—and perhaps Gods) whether I should go now:—the toss has decided I should not. On the contrary I am going to see Donne at Mattishall: a visit, which having put off a fortnight ago, I am now determined to pay. But if I do not see you before I go to London, I shall assuredly be down again by the latter part of February: when toasted cheese and ale shall again unite our souls. You need not however expect that I can return to such familiar intercourse as once (in former days) passed between us. New honours in society have devolved upon me the necessity of a more dignified deportment. A letter has been sent from the Secretary of the Ipswich Mechanics' Institution asking me to Lecture—any subject but Party Politics or Controversial Divinity. On my politely declining, another, a fuller, and a more pressing, letter was sent urging me to comply with their demand: I answered to the same effect, but with accelerated dignity. I am now awaiting the third request in confidence: if you see no symptoms of its being mooted, perhaps you will kindly propose it. I have prepared an answer. Donne is mad with envy. He consoles himself with having got a Roman History to write for Lardner's Cabinet Cyclopædia. What a pity it is that only Lying Histories are readable. I am afraid Donne will stick to what is considered the Truth too much.

This is a day like May: I and the children have been scrambling up and down the sides of a pit till our legs ache.

Jan. 24/42.

DEAR BARTON,

You mistake. The Poacher was bought in his shell—for £3—did I not name that price? As you desire a packing case, I will order one to day: and I hope you will have him down on Wednesday, just when your Bank work is over, and you will be glad of such good company. One of my friends thought the picture must have been an anticipation of Bill Sykes: put a cap and feathers on his head and you make him Iago, Richard the Third, or any other aristocratic villain. I really think the picture is a very good one of its kind: and one that you will like.[1]

I am going to get my large Constable very lightly framed, and shall bring it down into Suffolk with me to shew you and others. I like it more and more.

To F. Tennyson.

LONDON, *February* 6, 1842.

DEAR FREDERIC,

These fast-following letters of mine seem intended to refute a charge made against me by Morton: that I had only so much impulse of correspondence as resulted from the receipt of a friend's letter. Is it very frivolous to write all these letters, on no business whatsoever? What I think is, that one will soon be going into the country, where one hears no music, and sees no pictures, and so one will have nothing to write about. I mean to take down a Thucydides, to feed on : like a whole Parmesan. But at present here I am in London : last night I went to see Acis and Galatea brought out, with Handel's music, and Stanfield's scenery : really the best done thing I have seen for many a year. As I sat alone (alone in spirit) in the pit, I wished for you : and now Sunday is over : I have been to church : I have dined at Portland Place : [1] and now I come home to my lodgings : light my pipe : and will whisper something over to Italy. You talk of your Naples : and that one cannot understand Theocritus without having been on those shores. I tell you, you can't understand Macready without coming to London and seeing his revival of Acis and Galatea. You enter Drury Lane at a quarter to seven : the pit is already nearly full : but you find a seat, and a very pleasant one. Box doors open and shut : ladies take off their shawls and seat themselves : gentlemen twist their side curls : the musicians come up from under the stage one by one : 'tis just upon seven : Macready is very punctual : Mr. T. Cooke is in his place with his marshal's baton in his hand : he lifts it up : and off they set with old Handel's noble overture. As it is playing, the red velvet curtain (which Macready has substituted, not wisely, for the old green one) draws apart : and you see a rich drop scene, all festooned and arabesqued with River Gods, Nymphs,

[1] No. 39, where his father and mother lived.

and their emblems; and in the centre a delightful, large, good copy of Poussin's great landscape (of which I used to have a print in my rooms) where the Cyclops is seen seated on a mountain, looking over the sea-shore. The overture ends, the drop scene rises, and there is the sea-shore, a long curling bay: the sea heaving under the moon, and breaking upon the beach, and rolling the surf down —the stage! This is really capitally done. But enough of description. The choruses were well sung, well acted, well dressed, and well grouped; and the whole thing creditable and pleasant. Do you know the music? It is of Handel's best: and as classical as any man who wore a full-bottomed wig could write. I think Handel never gets out of his wig: that is, out of his age: his Hallelujah chorus is a chorus not of angels, but of well-fed earthly choristers, ranged tier above tier in a Gothic cathedral, with princes for audience, and their military trumpets flourishing over the full volume of the organ. Handel's gods are like Homer's, and his sublime never reaches beyond the region of the clouds. Therefore I think that his great marches, triumphal pieces, and coronation anthems, are his finest works. There is a little bit of Auber's, at the end of the Bayadère when the God resumes his divinity and retires into the sky, which has more of pure light and mystical solemnity than anything I know of Handel's: but then this is only a scrap: and Auber could not breathe in that atmosphere long: whereas old Handel's coursers, with necks with

thunder clothed and long resounding pace, never
tire. Beethoven thought more deeply also : but I
don't know if he could sustain himself so well. I
suppose you will resent this praise of Beethoven : but
you must be tired of the whole matter, written as it is
in this vile hand : and so here is an end of it. . . .
And now I am going to put on my night-cap : for my
paper is nearly ended, and the iron tongue of St.
Paul's, as reported by an East wind, has told · twelve.
This is the last news from the city. So Good night.
I suppose the violets will be going off in the Papal
dominions by the time this letter reaches you : my
country cousins are making much of a few aconites.
Love to Morton.

P.S. I hope these foolish letters don't cost you
and Morton much : I always pay 1s. 7d. for them
here : which ought to carry such levities to Hindostan
without further charge.

To Bernard Barton.

LONDON, *Febr.* 25/42.

MY DEAR BARTON,

Your reason for liking your Paul Veronese (what
an impudence to talk so to a man who has just
purchased a real Titian !) does not quite disprove my
theory. You like the picture because you like the
verses you once made upon it : you associate the
picture (naturally enough) with them : and so shall I

29

in future, because I like the verses too. But then you ask further, what made you write the verses if you were not moved by the picture imprimis? Why you know the poetic faculty does wonders, as Shakespeare tells us, in imagining the forms of things unseen, etc., and so you made a merit where there was none: and have liked that merit ever since. But I will not disturb you any further in your enjoyment: if you have a vision of your own, why should I undo it.?

Yesterday I was busily employed in painting over my Opie, which had suffered by heat, or something of that kind. I borrowed Laurence's palette and brushes and lay upon the floor two hours patching over and renovating. The picture is really greatly improved, and I am more reconciled to it. It has now to be varnished: and then I hope some fool will be surprised into giving £4 for it, as I did. I have selected an advantageous position for it in a dealer's shop, just under a rich window that excludes the light.

On second thoughts I shall not send you down my Twilight: but bring it with me. I like it much, and do not repent the purchase. As to the difficulty of bringing down so many pictures, I shall travel by the steamer; which will bear any quantity. The great new purchase, spoken of in yesterday's letter, will also go with me: it will be insured at a high valuation before it is entrusted to the Deep, of whose treasures I don't at all wish it to become one. My Titian is a great hit : if not by him, it is as near him as ever was painted. But you would not care six straws for it. The history of the finest theory of colouring lies in those few inches of canvas. But Laurence (who has gone for some days into the country) must see it, and tell me about it. He is so good a judge, that I ought never to talk till I have first heard his verdict.

I was amused at a passage in Clarissa the other day, which gives one some idea of what the average state of the arts was among the gentry of a hundred years ago. Miss Howe, in drawing up a character of her lost Clarissa, says that among other things she had a fine taste for the Pencil : had not time to practise it much, but 'was an absolute mistress of the " should be," ' and then proceeds thus : ' To give a familiar instance for the sake of young Ladies : she (untaught) observed *when but a child*, that the Sun, Moon, and Stars, never appeared at once : and were therefore never to be in one piece : that bears, tygers, lions, were not natives of an English climate, and should not therefore have a place in an English landscape : that these ravagers of the forest consorted not with lambs, kids, or fawns : nor kites, hawks, or vultures, with doves, partridges, and pheasants.' Such was a prodigy in those days. It is easy to sneer at this passage : but whoever has read anything of the Masques, etc., of James's time, will readily recall what absurdities were brought together, even by the good Scholars of the day : and therefore will not wonder at the imperfect Natural History that was found in young Ladies' Drawings, and samplers. I remember now to have seen wonderful combinations of phenomena in those samplers which are occasionally to be found hung up in the parlours of Country Inns, and Farm houses.

These letters succeed like the ghosts of Banquo's progeny before the eyes of Macbeth. Lucky that time itself draws on too close for this letter to 'hold a glass that shews you many more.' You did not answer my question about the Gainsboroughs. So I won't ask you another.

Sonnet on my new Picture.

Oh Twilight! Twilight!!

Rot me, if I am in a poetical humour: I can't translate the picture into words.

London, *March* 5, 1842.

My dear Barton,

Before the cavalcade and suite of Hardinge's (a melancholy procession) reaches you, I think this letter will. You need not envy me my purchases, which are imprudent ones: both because I can't well afford them, and because I have no house to put them. And yet all this gives a sense of stolen enjoyment to them. I am yet haunted with the ghost of a Battle-piece (little in my way) at a shop in Holborn: by whom I know not: but so good as to be cheap at

£4 : 10s., which the man wants for it. My Twilight *is* an upright picture : about a foot wide, and rather more than a foot high.

Mr. Browne has declined taking my Opie, unless in conjunction with some others which I won't part with : so the Forest Girl must set up ,her stall at a Broker's. I doubt she will never bring me the money I gave for her. She is the only bad speculation of the season. Were she but sold, I should be rejoicing in the Holborn Battle Piece. After this year however I think I shall bid complete adieu to picture-*hunting* : only taking what comes in my way. There is a great difference between these two things : both in the expense of time, thought, and money. Who can sit down to Plato while his brains are roaming to Holborn, Christie's, Phillips's, etc. ?

To F. Tennyson.

[31 *March*, 1842.]

DEAR FREDERIC,

. . . Concerning the bagwigs of composers. Handel's was not a bagwig, which was simply so named from the little stuffed black silk watch-pocket that hung down behind the back of the wearer. Such were Haydn's and Mozart's—much less influential or the character : much less ostentatious in themselves : not towering so high, nor rolling down in following curls so low as to overlay the nature of the brain within. But Handel wore the Sir Godfrey Kneller

33

wig: greatest of wigs: one of which some great General of the day used to take off his head after the fatigue of the battle, and hand over to his valet to have the bullets combed out of it. Such a wig as a fugue in itself. I don't understand your theory about trumpets, which have always been so little spiritual *in use*, that they have been the provocatives and celebrators of physical force from the beginning of the world. '*Power*,' whether spiritual or physical, is the meaning of the trumpet: and so, well used, as you say, by Handel in his approaches to the Deity. The fugue in the overture to the Messiah expresses perhaps the thorny wandering ways of the world before the voice of the one in the wilderness, and before 'Comfort ye my people, etc.' Mozart, I agree with you, is the most universal musical genius: Beethoven has been too analytical and erudite: but his inspiration is nevertheless true. I have just read his Life by Moscheles: well worth reading. He shewed no very decided preference for music when a child, though he was the son of a composer: and I think that he was, strictly speaking, more of a thinker than a musician. A great genius he was somehow. He was very fond of reading: Plutarch and Shakespeare his great favourites. He tried to think in music: almost to reason in music: whereas perhaps we should be contented with *feeling* in it. It can never speak very definitely. There is that famous 'Holy, Holy, Lord God Almighty, etc.,' in Handel: nothing can sound more simple and devotional: but

34

it is only lately adapted to these words, being originally (I believe) a love song in Rodelinda. Well, lovers adore their mistresses more than their God. Then the famous music of ' He layeth the beams of his chambers in the waters, etc.,' was originally fitted to an Italian pastoral song—' Nasce al bosco in rozza cuna, un felice pastorello, etc.' That part which seems so well to describe 'and walketh on the wings of the wind ' falls happily in with ' e con l'aura di fortuna ' with which this pastorello sailed along. The character of the music is ease and largeness : as the shepherd lived, so God Almighty walked on the wind. The music breathes ease : but words must tell us who takes it easy. Beethoven's Sonata—Op. 14—is meant to express the discord and gradual atonement of two lovers, or a man and his wife : and he was disgusted that every one did not see what was meant : in truth, it expresses any resistance gradually overcome—Dobson shaving with a blunt razor, for instance. Music is so far the most universal language, that any one piece in a particular strain symbolizes all the analogous phenomena spiritual or material—if you can talk of spiritual phenomena. The Eroica symphony describes the battle of the passions as well as of armed men. This is long and muddy discourse : but the walls of Charlotte Street present little else, especially during this last week of Lent, to twaddle about. The Cambridge Dons have been up in town for the Easter vacation : so we have smoked and talked over Peacock, Whewell, etc. Alfred is busy preparing a new volume for the press : full of doubts, troubles, etc. The reviewers will doubtless be at him : and with justice for many things : but some of the poems will outlive the reviewers.

BEDFORD, *August* 16, 1842.

DEAR TENNYSON,

I have been long hoping for a letter from you : it has come this morning, and repays me for all waiting. While you and Morton write to me about Italy I shall never go to see it. And yet your account of Cicero's villa, I confess, gives me a twinge. But of this I am sure : if I saw all these fine things with the bodily eye, I should but see them as a scene in a play, with the additional annoyance of being bitten with fleas perhaps, and being in a state of transition which is not suitable to me : whereas while you see them, and will represent them to me, I see them through your imagination, and that is better than any light of my own. This is very true, I assure you : and you and Morton have given me quite a different view of Italy to what I had before : a much more enchanting one, but not the more likely to seduce me into making the false step of trying to realize it for myself. . . . In the mean time how tired and bored would you be to take one of my travels —a voyage of eight miles from Bedford perhaps—

travelled twenty times before—every winding of the river, every church-spire, every country pot house and the quality of its beer, well known. No surprise at all. Nil admirari—I find that old Horace is a good fellow-traveller in England : so is Virgil. It is odd that those fellows living in the land they did live in should have talked so coldly about it. As to Alfred's book, I believe it has sold well : but I have not seen him for a long while, and have had no means of hearing about the matter except from Thompson, who told me that very many copies had been sold at Cambridge, which indeed will be the chief market for them. Neither have I seen any notice of them in print except that in the Examiner ; and that seemed so quiet that I scarce supposed it was by Forster. Alfred himself is, I believe, in Kent at present. And now, my dear Frederic, why do you think of returning to England ? Depend upon it you are better off as you are. You will never turn magistrate nor bean-dibbler, nor make yourself of use in the country, and therefore why should you not live where you like to live best ? When I read of your laughing and singing and riding into Naples with huge self-supplying beakers full of the warm South I am sure you had best stay where you are. I should indeed be very glad to see you again : but then I should miss hearing from you : and you would only come here to abuse us all and go back again. You Tennysons are born for warm climates. As to poor England, I never see a paper, but I think with you that she is on the go. I used to dread this : but somehow I now contemplate it as a necessary thing, and, till the shoe begins to pinch me sorely, walk on with some indifference. It seems impossible the manufacturers can go on as they are : and impossible that the demand for our goods can continue as of old in Europe : and impossible but that we must get a rub and licking in some of our colonies : and if all these things come at once, why then the devil's in it. I used to think as you do about France and the French : and we all agreed in London that France should be divided among the other powers as Poland was : but Donne has given me pause : he says that France is the great counteracting democratic principle to Russia. This may be : though I think Russia is too unwieldly and rotten-ripe ever to make a huge progress in conquest. What is to be thought of a nation where the upper classes speak the language of another country, and have varnished over their honest barbarism with the poorest French profligacy and intrigue? Russia does not seem a whole to me. In the mean time, all goes on toward better and better, as is my firm belief : and humanity grows clear by flowing, (very little profited by any single sage or hero), and man shall have wings to fly and something much better than that in the end. . . .

I draw a very little, and think of music as I walk in the fields : but have no piano in this part of the world. . . . I hear there is a fine new Symphony by Mendelssohn, who is by far our best writer now, and in some measure combines Beethoven and Handel. I grow every day more and more to love only the old God save the King style : the common chords, those truisms of music, like other truisms so little understood in the full. Just look at the mechanism of Robin Adair.

Now pray write to me again when you can. You don't know how much I rejoice in your letters.

To S. Laurence.

BEDFORD, *Thursday,*
[*August,* 1842.]

DEAR LAURENCE,

. . . I have heard from Morton and F. Tennyson ; the letter of the latter very descriptive and fine. He is summering at Castellamare, and Morton at Sorrento. What must Italy be if we are complaining of heat here !

I have just been naming all Mr. Browne's pictures for him. This he has insisted on for three years, and at last this very hot day after an early dinner pens and paper were brought out and I have been writing down awful calumnies about Cuyp, Both, etc. Who could have painted Catharine of Medicis, do you know ? We are afraid to call it Vandyke, as he lived (I believe) a century after her : and Mr. B. won't give up its being Catharine's portrait. So here we are in a fix. I went to see Lord Northampton's place Castle Ashby a week ago : expected pictures, and saw very bad ones. The house is very handsome, built by Inigo Jones.

I weigh 14 stone—fact.

To F. Tennyson.

BOULGE HALL, WOODBRIDGE,
Sunday, Dec. 10/1843.

DEAR FREDERIC,

Either you wrote me word yourself, or some one told me, that you meant to winter at Florence. So I shall direct to the Poste Restante there. You see I am not settled at the Florence of Suffolk, called Ipswich, yet : but I am perhaps as badly off; being in this most dull country house quite alone ; a grey mist, that seems teeming with half formed snow, all over the landscape before my windows. It is also Sunday morning : ten of the clock by the chime now sounding from the stables. I have fed on bread and milk (a dreadfully opaque diet) and I await the morning Church in humble hope. It will begin in half an hour. We keep early hours in the country. So you will be able exactly to measure my aptitude and fullness for letter writing by the quantity written now, before I bolt off for hat, gloves, and prayerbook. I always put on my thickest great coat to go to our Church in : as fungi grow in great numbers about the communion table. And now, to turn away from Boulge, I must tell you that I went up to London a month ago to see old Thackeray, who had come there to have his eyes doctored. I stayed with him ten days and we were as usual together. Alfred came up 'in transitu' from Boxley to Cheltenham; he looked, and said he was, ill: I have never seen him so hopeless: and I am really anxious to know how he is. . . . I remember the days of the summer when you and I were together, quarrelling and laughing —these I remember with pleasure. Our trip to Gravesend has left a perfume with me. I can get up with you on that everlastingly stopping coach on which we tried to travel from Gravesend to Maidstone that Sunday morning: worn out with it, we got down at an inn, and then got up on another coach—and an old smiling fellow passed us holding out his hat—and you said, 'That old fellow must go about as Homer did'—and numberless other turns of road and humour, which sometimes pass before me as I lie in bed. . . . Now before I turn over, I will go and see about Church, as I hear no bell, pack myself up as warmly as I can, and be off. So good-bye till twelve o'clock. —'Tis five minutes past twelve by the stable clock: so I saw as I returned from Church through the garden. Parson and Clerk got through the service see saw like two men in a sawpit. In the garden I see the heads of the snowdrops and crocuses just out of the earth. Another year with its same flowers and topics to open upon us. Shenstone somewhere sings,[1]

[1] Elegy xi.

41

> Tedious again to mark the drizzling day,
>   Again to trace the same sad tracts of snow :
> Or, lull'd by vernal airs, again survey
>   The selfsame hawthorn bud, and cowslips blow.

I rely on you and all your family sympathizing in this. So do I sometimes : anyhow, people complimenting each other on the approach of Spring and such like felicitations are very tiresome. Our very year is of a paltry diameter. But this is not proper language for Mark Tapley, whose greatest bore just now is having a bad pen ; but the letter is ended. So he is jolly and yours as ever.

BOULGE, WOODBRIDGE, *February* 24/44.

MY DEAR FREDERIC,

I got your letter all right. But you did not tell me where to direct to you again ; so I must send to the Poste Restante at Florence. I have also heard from Morton, to whom I despatched a letter yesterday: and now set about one to you. As you live in two different cities, one may write about the same things to both. You told me of the Arno being frozen, and even Italian noses being cold : he tells me the Spring is coming. I tell you that we have had the mildest winter known ; but as good weather, when it does come in England, is always unseasonable, and as an old proverb says that a green Yule makes a fat kirkyard, so it has been with us : the extraordinary fine season has killed heaps of people with influenza, debilitated others for their lives long, worried everybody with colds, etc. I have had three influenzas: but this is no wonder: for I live in a hut with walls as thin as a sixpence: windows that don't shut: a clay soil safe beneath my feet: a thatch perforated by lascivious sparrows over my head. Here I sit, read, smoke, and become very wise, and am already quite beyond earthly things. I must say to you, as Basil Montagu once said, in perfect charity, to his friends: 'You see, my dear fellows, I like you very much, but I continue to advance, and you remain where you are (you see), and so I shall be obliged to leave you behind me. It is no fault of mine.' You must begin to read Seneca, whose letters I have been reading: else, when you come back to England, you will be no companion to a man who despises wealth, death, etc. What are pictures but paintings—what are auctions but sales! All is vanity. Erige animum tuum, mî Lucili, etc. I wonder whether old Seneca was indeed such a humbug as people now say he was: he is really a fine writer. About three hundred years ago, or less, our divines and writers called him the divine Seneca; and old Bacon is full of him. One sees in him the upshot of all the Greek philosophy, how it stood in Nero's time, when the Gods had worn out a good deal. I don't think old Seneca believed he should live again. Death is his great resource. Think of the *rococity* of a gentleman studying Seneca in the middle of February 1844 in a remarkably damp cottage.

I have heard from Alfred also, who hates his water life—βίος ἄβιος he calls it—but hopes to be cured in March. Poor fellow, I trust he may. He is not in a happy plight, I doubt. I wish I lived in a pleasant country where he might like to come and stay with me—but this is one of the ugliest places in England—one of the dullest—it has not the merit of being bleak on a grand scale—pollard trees over a flat clay, with regular hedges. I saw a stanza in an old book which seemed to describe my condition rather—

> Far from thy kyn cast thee :
> Wrath not thy neighbour next thee,
> In a good corn country rest thee,
> And sit down, Robin, and rest thee.[1]

Funny advice, isn't it ? I am glad to hear Septimus is so much improved. I beg you will felicitate him from me : I have a tacit regard of the true sort for him, as I think I must have for all of the Tennyson build. I see so many little natures about that I must draw to the large, even if their faults be on the same scale as their virtues. You and I shall I suppose quarrel as often as we meet : but I can quarrel and never be the worse with you. How we pulled against each other at Gravesend ! You would stay—I wouldn't—then I would—then we did. Do you remember the face of that girl at the Bazaar, who kept talking to us and looking all round the room for fresh customers—a way women have—that is, a way

[1] Reliquiæ Antiquæ, i. 233.

44

of doing rather gracefully ? Then the gentleman who sang Ivy green; a very extraordinary accentuation, it seemed to me: but I believe you admired it very much. Really, if these little excursions in the company of one's friends leave such a pleasant taste behind in the memory, one should court them oftener. And yet then perhaps the relish would grow less: it is the infrequency that gives them room to expand. I shall never get to Italy, that seems clear. My great travel this year will be to Carlisle. Quid prosit ista tua longa peregrinatio, etc. Travelling, you know, is a vanity. The *soul* remains the same. An amorem possis fugare, an libidinis exsiccari, an timorem mortis depellere ? What then will you say to Pollock's being married ! I hear he is to be. Ad matrimonium fugis ? Miser ! Scævola noster dicere solebat, etc. Excuse my overflowing with philosophy. I am going this evening to eat toasted cheese with that celebrated poet Bernard Barton. And I must soon stir, and look about for my great coat, brush myself, etc. It blows a harrico, as Theodore Hook used to say, and will rain before I get to Woodbridge. Those poor mistaken lilac buds there out of the window ! and an old Robin, ruffled up to his thickest, sitting mournfully under them, quite disheartened. For you must know the mild winter is just giving way to a remarkably severe spring. . . . I wish you were here to smoke a pipe with me. I play of evenings some of Handel's great choruses which are the bravest music after all. I am getting to the true John Bull style of music. I delight in Handel's Allegro and Penseroso. Do you know the fine pompous joyous chorus of 'These pleasures, Mirth, if thou canst give, etc.' ? Handel certainly does in music what old Bacon desires in his Essay on Masques, 'Let the songs be loud and cheerful, not puling, etc.' One might think the Water music was written from this text.

To Bernard Barton.

19 CHARLOTTE ST.. *April* 11/44.

DEAR BARTON,

I am still indignant at this nasty place London. Thackeray, whom I came up to see, went off to Brighton the night after I arrived, and has not re-appeared : but I must wait some time longer for him. Thank Miss Barton much for the *kit ;* if it is but a kit : my old woman is a great lover of cats, and hers has just *kitted*, and a wretched little blind puling tabby lizard of a thing was to be saved from the pail for me : but if Miss Barton's is *a kit*, I will gladly have it : and my old lady's shall be disposed of—not to the pail. Oh rus, quando te aspiciam ? Construe that, Mr. Barton.—I am going to send down my pictures to Boulge, if I can secure them : they are not quite secure at present. If they vanish, I snap my fingers at them, Magi and all—there is a world (alas !) else-where beyond pictures—Oh, oh, oh, oh—

I smoked a pipe with Carlyle yesterday. We

ascended from his dining room carrying pipes and tobacco up through two stories of his house, and got into a little dressing room near the roof : there we sat down : the window was open and looked out on nursery gardens, their almond trees in blossom, and beyond, bare walls of houses, and over these, roofs and chimneys, and roofs and chimneys, and here and there a steeple, and whole London crowned with darkness gathering behind like the illimitable resources of a dream. I tried to persuade him to leave the accursed den, and he wished—but—but—perhaps he *didn't* wish on the whole.

When I get back to Boulge I shall recover my quietude which is now all in a ripple. But it is a shame to talk of such things. So Churchyard has caught another Constable. Did he get off our Debach boy that set the shed on fire ? Ask him that. Can'st thou not minister to a mind diseased, etc.

A cloud comes over Charlotte Street and seems as if it were sailing softly on the April wind to fall in a blessed shower upon the lilac buds and thirsty anemones somewhere in Essex.; or, who knows ?, perhaps at Boulge. Out will run Mrs. Faiers, and with red arms and face of woe haul in the struggling windows of the cottage, and make all tight. Beauty Bob[1] will cast a bird's eye out at the shower, and bless the useful wet. Mr. Loder will observe to the farmer for whom he is doing up a dozen of Queen's Heads, that it will be of great use : and the farmer

[1] His parrot.

will agree that his young barleys wanted it much. The German Ocean will dimple with innumerable pin points, and porpoises rolling near the surface sneeze with unusual pellets of fresh water—

> Can such things be,
> And overcome us like a summer cloud,
> Without our special wonder?

Oh this wonderful wonderful world, and we who stand in the middle of it are all in a maze, except poor Matthews of Bedford, who fixes his eyes upon a wooden Cross and has no misgiving whatsoever. When I was at his chapel on Good Friday, he called at the end of his grand sermon on some of the people to say merely this, that they believed Christ had redeemed them : and first one got up and in sobs declared she believed it : and then another, and then another—I was quite overset :—all poor people : how much richer than all who fill the London Churches. Theirs is the kingdom of Heaven !

This is a sad farrago.   Farewell.

To F. Tennyson.

BOULGE, WOODBRIDGE,
May 24/44.

MY DEAR FREDERIC,

I think you mean never to write to me again.   But you should, for I enjoy your letters much for years after I have got them.   They tell me all I shall know of Italy, beside many other good things.   I received one letter from you from Florence, and as you gave me no particular direction, I wrote to you at the Poste Restante there. I am now inditing this letter on the same venture. As my location is much more permanent, I command you to respond to me the very day you get this, warmed into such faint inspiration as my turnip radiance can kindle. You have seen a turnip lantern perhaps. Well, here I continue to exist: having broken my rural vegetation by one month in London, where I saw all the old faces — some only in passing, however — saw as few sights as possible, leaving London two days before the Exhibition opened. This is not out of moroseness or love of singularity: but I really supposed there could be nothing new: and therefore the best way would [be] to come new to it oneself after three or four years absence. I see in Punch a humorous catalogue of supposed pictures; Prince Albert's favourite spaniel and boot-jack, the Queen's Macaw with a Muffin, etc., by Landseer, etc., in which I recognize Thackeray's fancy. He is in full vigour play and pay in London, writing in a dozen reviews, and a score of newspapers: and while health lasts he sails before the wind. I have not heard of Alfred since March. . . . Spedding devotes his days to Lord Bacon in the British Museum: his nights to the usual profligacy. . . . My dear Frederic, you must select some of your poems and publish them: we want some bits of strong genuine imagination to help put to flight these——etc. Publish a book of fragments, if nothing else but single lines, or else the whole poems. When will you come to England and do it? I dare say I should have stayed longer in London had you been there: but the wits were too much for me. Not Spedding, mind: who is a dear fellow. But one finds few in London *serious* men: I mean *serious* even in fun: with a true purpose and character whatsoever it may be. London melts away all individuality into a common lump of cleverness. I am amazed at the humour and worth and noble feeling in the country, however much railroads have mixed us up with metropolitan civilization. I can still find the heart of England beating healthily down here, though no one will believe it.

You know my way of life so well that I need not describe it to you, as it has undergone no change since I saw you. I read of mornings; the same old books over and over again, having no command of new ones: walk with my great black dog of an afternoon, and at evening sit with open windows, up to which China roses climb, with my pipe, while the blackbirds and thrushes begin to rustle bedwards in the garden, and the nightingale to have the neighbourhood to herself. We have had such a spring (bating the last ten days) as would have satisfied even you with warmth. And such verdure! white clouds moving over the new fledged tops of oak trees, and acres of grass striving with buttercups. How old to tell of, how new to see ! I believe that Leslie's Life of Constable (a very charming book) has given me a fresh love of Spring. Constable loved it above all seasons : he hated Autumn. When Sir G. Beaumont who was of the old classical taste asked him if he did not find it difficult to place *his brown tree* in his pictures, 'Not at all,' said C., 'I never put one in at all.' And when Sir George was crying up the tone of the old masters' landscapes, and quoting an *old violin* as the proper tone of colour for a picture, Constable got up, took an old Cremona, and laid it down on the sunshiny grass. You would like the book. In defiance of all this, I have hung my room with pictures, like very old fiddles indeed : but I agree with Sir George and Constable both. I like pictures that are not like nature. I can have nature better than any picture by looking out of my window. Yet I respect the man who tries to paint up to the freshness of earth and sky. Constable did not wholly achieve what he tried at : and perhaps the old masters chose a soberer scale of things as more within the compass of lead paint. To paint dew with lead !

I also plunge away at my old Handel of nights, and delight in the Allegro and Penseroso, full of pomp and fancy. What a pity Handel could not have written music to some great Masque, such as Ben Jonson or Milton would have written, if they had known of such a musician to write for.

To Bernard Barton.

19 CHARLOTTE ST.,
RATHBONE PLACE.
[1844.]

DEAR BARTON,

...I heard a man preach at Bedford in a way that shook my soul. He described the crucifixion in a way that put the scene before his people — no fine words, and metaphors : but first one nail struck into one hand, and then into another, and one through both feet—the cross lifted up with God in man's image distended upon it. And the sneers of the priests below—'Look at that fellow there—look at him—he talked of saving others, etc.' And then the sun veiled his face in Blood, etc. I certainly have heard oratory now — of the Lord Chatham kind, only Matthews has more faith in Christ than Pitt in his majority. I was almost as much taken aback as the poor folks all about me who sobbed : and I hate this beastly London more and more. It stinks all through of churchyards and fish shops. As to pictures—well, never mind them. Farewell !

To F. Tennyson.

BOULGE, WOODBRIDGE, *Dec^r.* 8/44.

MY DEAR FREDERIC,

. . .It is very smooth sailing hitherto down here. No velvet waistcoat and ever-lustrous pumps to be considered ; no bon mots got up ; no information necessary. There is a pipe for the parsons to smoke, and quite as much bon mots, literature, and philosophy as they care for without any trouble at all. If we could but feed our poor! It is now the 8th of December; it has blown a most desperate East wind, all razors; a wind like one of those knives one sees at shops in London, with 365 blades all drawn and pointed; the wheat is all sown; the fallows cannot be ploughed. What are all the poor folks to do during the winter? And they persist in having the same enormous families they used to do; a woman came to me two days ago who had seventeen children! What farmers are to employ all these? What Landlord can find room for them? The law of Generation must be repealed. The London press does nothing but rail at us poor country folks for our cruelty. I am glad they do so; for there is much to be set right. But I want to know if the Editor of the Times is more attentive to his devils, their wives and families, than our squires and squiresses and parsons are to their fellow parishioners. Punch also assumes a tone of virtuous satire, from the mouth of Mr. Douglas Jerrold! It is easy to sit in arm chairs at a club in Pall Mall and rail on the stupidity and brutality of those in High Suffolk....

P.S. Next morning. Snow over the ground. We have our wonders of inundation in Suffolk also, I can tell you. For three weeks ago such floods came, that an old woman was carried off as she was retiring from a beer house about 9 p.m., and drowned. She was probably half seas over before she left the beer house.

And three nights ago I looked out at about ten o'clock at night, before going to bed. It seemed perfectly still; frosty, and the stars shining bright. I heard a continuous moaning sound, which I knew to be, not that of an infant exposed, or female ravished, but of the sea, more than ten miles off! What little wind there was carried to us the murmurs of the waves circulating round these coasts so far over a flat country. But people here think that this sound so heard is not from the waves that break, but a kind of prophetic voice from the body of the sea itself announcing great gales. Sure enough we have got them, however heralded. Now I say that all this shows that we in this Suffolk are not so completely given over to prose and turnips as some would have us. I always said that being near the sea, and being able to catch a glimpse of it from the tops of hills, and of houses, redeemed Suffolk from dullness; and at all events that our turnip fields, dull in themselves, were at least set all round with an undeniably poetic element. And so I see Arnold says; he enumerates five inland counties as the only parts of England for which nothing could be said in praise. Not that I agree with him there neither; I cannot allow the valley of the Ouse about which some of my pleasantest recollections hang to be without its great charm. W. Browne, whom you despised, is married, and I shall see but little of him for the future. I have laid by

my rod and line by the willows of the Ouse for ever.
'He is married ,and cannot come.' This change is
the true meaning of those verses,[1]

> Friend after friend departs ;
> Who has not lost a friend ?

and so on. If I were conscious of being stedfast and
good humoured enough, I would marry to-morrow.
But a humourist is best by himself.

To Bernard Barton.

GELDESTONE, *April* 3/45.

MY DEAR BARTON,

. . . I have been loitering out in the garden here this
golden day of Spring. The woodpigeons coo in the
covert; the frogs croak in the pond; the bees hum
about some thyme, and some of my smaller nieces
have been busy gathering primroses, 'all to make
posies suitable to this present month.' I cannot but
think with a sort of horror of being in London now :
but I doubt I must be ere long. . . . I have abjured
all Authorship, contented at present with the divine
Poem which Great Nature is now composing about
us. These primroses seem more wonderful and
delicious Annuals than Ackerman ever put forth. I
suppose no man ever grew so old as not to feel

[1] By James Montgomery : 'Friends' in his Miscellaneous Poems
(Works, ii. 298, ed. 1836).

younger in Spring. Yet, poor old Mrs. Bodham [1] lifted up her eyes to the windows, and asked if it were a clear or a dull day !

39 NORTON ST., FITZROY SQR.
[? *May* 1845.]

DEAR BARTON,

You see my address. I only got into it yesterday, though I reached London on Friday, and hung loose upon it for all that interval. I spent four days at Cambridge pleasantly enough ; and one at Bedford where I heard my friend Matthews preach.

Last night I appeared at the Opera, and shall do so twice a week till further notice. Friends I have seen but few ; for I have not yet found time to do anything. Alfred Tennyson was here ; but went off yesterday to consider the sea from the top of Beachy Head. Carlyle gets on with his book which will be in two big volumes. He has entirely misstated all about Naseby, after all my trouble. . . .

Did Churchyard see in London a picture at the address I enclose ? The man's card, you see, proclaims 'Silversmith,' but he is 'Pawnbroker.' A picture hangs up at the door which he calls by 'Williams,' but I think is a rather inferior Crome ; though the figure in it is not like Crome's figures. The picture is about three feet high by two broad ;

---

[1] Great aunt of W. B. Donne.

good in the distance; very natural in the branching of the trees; heavy in the foliage; all common to Crome. And it seems painted in that fat substance he painted in. If C. come to London let him look at this picture, as well as come and see me.

I have cold, head-ache, and London disgust. Oh that I could look on my Anemones! and hear the sighing of my Scotch firs. The Exhibition is full of bad things: there is a grand Turner, however; quite unlike anything that was ever seen in Heaven above, or in Earth beneath, or in the waters under the Earth.

The reign of primroses and cowslips is over, and the oak now begins to take up the empire of the year and wear a budding garland about his brows. Over all this settles down the white cloud in the West, and the Morning and Evening draw toward Summer.

To F. Tennyson.

BOULGE, WOODBRIDGE.
[After *Sept.* 1845.]

MY DEAR FREDERIC,

I do beg and desire that when you next begin a letter to me you will not tear it up (as you say you have done some) because of its exhibiting a joviality insulting to any dumps of mine. What was I complaining of so? I forget all about it. It seems to me to be two years since I heard from you. If you had said that my answers to your letters were so barren as to dishearten you from deserving any more I should understand that very well. But if you really did accomplish any letters and not send them, I say, a fico for thy friendship! Do so no more. . . .

The finale of C minor is very noble. I heard it twice at Jullien's. On the whole I like to hear Mozart better; Beethoven is gloomy. Besides incontestably Mozart is the purest *musician*; Beethoven would have been Poet or Painter as well, for he had a great deep Soul and Imagination. I do not think it is reported that he showed any very early predilection for Music; Mozart, we know, did. They say Holmes has published a very good life of M. Only think of the poor fellow not being able to sell his music latterly, getting out of fashion, so taking to drink . . . and enact Harlequin at Masquerades! When I heard Handel's Alexander's Feast at Norwich this Autumn I wondered; but when directly afterward they played Mozart's G minor Symphony, it seemed as if I had passed out of a land of savages into sweet civilized Life.

To W. F. Pollock.

BOULGE. WOODBRIDGE,
Wednesday [1846].

MY DEAR POLLOCK,

I was glad to hear from you; and I congratulate you on having secured stedfast office and revenue that will put you at ease, and end all trouble and

disappointment.[1]   Henceforth you may sit on your
bench and look down complacently on the *mare
magnum* of wigs all striving which shall rise topmost.
And, as you say, you can now set about finding out
what to do with much spare time ; a thing hard to do
at all times (how tiresome was a whole holiday at
school!), but most hard to men who have for the
greater part of their lives been accustomed to a
regular day-full of work.   And all must leave it at
some time.   I have been all my life apprentice to
this heavy business of idleness ; and am not yet
master of my craft ; the Gods are too just to suffer
that I should.

Since I saw you I have been here, except going
for a month to Bedford, and a fortnight to Cambridge.
At Cambridge I saw Thompson, whose mind is bunged
up with Lecture and Tutor work ; and Merivale, who
looks fat, and grows grey, and was quaint and
pleasant as usual.   I have seen no new books : and
have even neglected to get down my due box-full of
old ones from the London Library.   Have you seen
Festus ?   Tennyson writes word there are very fine
things in it.   He is come back from Switzerland
rather disappointed, I am glad to say.   How could
such herds of gaping idiots come back enchanted if
there were much worth going to see ?   I think that
tours in Switzerland and Italy are less often published
now than formerly : but there is all Turkey, Greece,

---

[1] In 1846 W. F. Pollock was made a Master of the Court of
Exchequer.

and the East to be prostituted also : and I fear we shan't hear the end of it in our lifetimes. Suffolk turnips seem to me so classical compared to all that sort of thing.

I believe I shall be in London shortly before, or after, Christmas : and shall assuredly look for you. Do you ever see Thackeray ? I read some pretty verses of his in Mrs. Norton's Drawing Room Scrap Book ; and *such* a copy of verses to her Ladyship by Sir Edward ! It is impossible to read verses worse in sense or sound. And how Mrs. Norton could admit such vulgar flattery ! I am afraid the Suffolk turnips are better than her too : and they are not particularly good this year.

To E. B. Cowell.

BEDFORD, *Septr.* 15/46.

DEAR COWELL,

Here I am at last, after making a stay at Lowestoft, where I sailed in boats, bathed, and in all ways enjoyed the sea air. I wished for you upon a heathy promontory there, good museum for conversation on old poets, etc. What have you been reading, and what tastes of rare Authors have you to send me ? I have read (as usual with me) but very little, what with looking at the sea with its crossing and recrossing ships, and dawdling with my nieces of an evening. Besides a book is to me what Locke says that watching the hour hand of a clock is to all; other thoughts (and those of the idlest and seemingly most irrelevant) will intrude between my vision and the written words : and then I have to read over again; often again and again till all is crossed and muddled. If Life were to be very much longer than is the usual lot of men, one would try very hard to reform this lax habit, and clear away such a system of gossamer association : even as it is, I try to turn all wandering fancy out of doors, and listen attentively to Whately's Logic, and old Spinoza still ! . . .

To S. Laurence.

GELDESTONE HALL, BECCLES.
[*June* 20, 1847.]

MY DEAR LAURENCE,

I have had another letter from the Bartons asking about your advent. In fact Barton's daughter is anxious for her Father's to be done, and done this year. He is now sixty - three ; and it won't do, you know, for grand - climacterical people to pro- crastinate — nay, to *proannuate* — which is a new, and, for all I see, a very bad word. But, be this as it may, do you come down to Woodbridge this summer if you can ; and that you can, I doubt not ; since it· is no great things out of your way to or from Norwich.

The means to get to Ipswich are — A steamboat will bring you for five shillings (a very pretty sail)

from the Custom House to Ipswich, the Orwell
steamer; going twice a week, and heard of directly
in the fishy latitudes of London Bridge. Or, a
railroad brings you for the same sum; if you will
travel third class, which I sometimes do in fine
weather. I should recommend *that;* the time
being so short, so certain : and no eating and
drinking by the way, as must be in a steamer.
At Ipswich, I pick you up with the washerwoman's
pony and take you to Woodbridge. There Barton
sits with the tea already laid out; and Miss about
to manage the urn; plain, agreeable people. At
Woodbridge too is my little friend Churchyard,
with whom we shall sup off toasted cheese and
porter. Then, last and not least, the sweet retire-
ment of Boulge : where the Graces and Muses, etc.

I write thus much because my friends seem
anxious; my friend, I mean, Miss Barton : for
Barton pretends he dreads having his portrait
done; which is 'my eye.' So come and do it.
He is a generous, worthy, simple - hearted, fellow :
worth ten thousand better wits. Then you shall
see all the faded tapestry of country town life :
London jokes worn threadbare ; third rate accom-
plishments infinitely prized ; scandal removed from
Dukes and Duchesses to the Parson, the Banker,
the Commissioner of Excise, and the Attorney.

Let me hear from you soon that you are coming.
I shall return to Boulge the end of this week.

P.S. Come if you can the latter part of the week; when the Quaker is most at leisure. There is a daily coach from Woodbridge to Norwich.

To Bernard Barton.

GLOUCESTER, *Augst.* 29/47.

MY DEAR BARTON,

. . . After I wrote to you at Exeter, I went for three days to the Devonshire coast; and then to Lusia's home in Somersetshire. I never saw her look better or happier. De Soyres pretty well; their little girl grown a pretty and strong child; their baby said to be very thriving. They live in a fine, fruitful, and picturesque country: green pastures, good arable, clothed with trees, bounded with hills that almost reach mountain dignity, and in sight of the Bristol Channel which is there all but Sea. I fancy the climate is moist, and I should think the trees are too many for health: but I was there too little time to quarrel with it on that score. After being there, I went to see a parson friend in Dorsetshire;[1] a quaint, humorous man. Him I found in a most out-of-the-way parish in a fine open country; not so much wooded; chalk hills. This man used to wander about the fields at Cambridge with me when we both wore caps and gowns, and then we proposed and discussed many ambitious schemes and subjects.

[1] Francis Duncan, rector of West Chelborough.

He is now a quiet, saturnine, parson with five children, taking a pipe to soothe him when they bother him with their noise or their misbehaviour: and I !—as the Bishop of London said, 'By the grace of God I am what I am.' In Dorsetshire I found the churches much occupied by Puseyite Parsons; new chancels built with altars, and painted windows that officiously displayed the Virgin Mary, etc. The people in those parts call that party 'Pugicides,' and receive their doctrine and doings peacefully. I am vext at these silly men who are dishing themselves and their church as fast as they can.

To F. Tennyson.

[LEAMINGTON, 4 *Sept.* 1847.]

MY DEAR FREDERIC,

I believe I must attribute your letter to your having skipped to Leghorn, and so got animated by the sight of a new place. *I* also am an Arcadian: have been to Exeter—the coast of Devonshire—the Bristol Channel—and to visit a Parson in Dorsetshire. He wore cap and gown when I did at Cambridge— together did we roam the fields about Granchester, discuss all things, thought ourselves fine fellows, and that one day we should make a noise in the world. He is now a poor Rector in one of the most out-of-the-way villages in England—has five children—fats and kills his pig—smokes his pipe—loves his home and cares not ever to be seen or heard of out of it. I was amused with his company; he much pleased to see me: we had not met face to face for fifteen years —and now both of us such very sedate unambitious people! Now I am verging homeward; taking Leamington and Bedford in my way. . . .

To T. Carlyle.

ALDERMAN BROWNE'S, BEDFORD.
[20 *Septr.* 1847.]

DEAR CARLYLE,

I was very glad of your letter: especially as regards that part in it about the Derbyshire villages. In many other parts of England (not to mention my own Suffolk) you would find the same substantial goodness among the people, resulting (as you say) from the funded virtues of many good humble men gone by. I hope you will continue to teach us all, as you have done, to make some use and profit of all this: at least, not to let what good remains to die away under penury and neglect. I also hope you will have some mercy now, and in future, on the 'Hebrew rags' which are grown offensive to you; considering that it was these rags that really did bind together those virtues which have transmitted down to us all the good you noticed in Derbyshire. If the old creed was so commendably effective in the Generals and Counsellors of two hundred years ago, I think we may be well content to let it work still among the ploughmen and weavers of to-day ; and even to suffer some absurdities in the Form, if the Spirit does well upon the whole. Even poor Exeter Hall ought, I think, to be borne with ; it is at least better than the wretched Oxford business. When I was in Dorset-shire some weeks ago, and saw chancels done up in sky-blue and gold, with niches, candles, an *Altar*, rails to keep off the profane laity, and the parson (like your Reverend Mr. Hitch [1]) *intoning* with his back to the people, I thought the Exeter Hall war-cry of 'The Bible—the whole Bible—and nothing but the Bible' a good cry : I wanted Oliver and his dragoons to march in and put an end to it all. Yet our Established Parsons (when quiet and in their senses) make good country gentlemen, and magistrates ; and I am glad to secure one man of means and education in each parish of England : the people can always resort to Wesley, Bunyan, and Baxter, if they want stronger food than the old Liturgy, and the orthodox Discourse. I think you will not read what I have written : or be very bored with it. But it *is* written now.

To E. B. Cowell.

[1847]

DEAR COWELL,

. . . I am only got half way in the third book of Thucydides : but I go on with pleasure ; with as much

---

[1] See Carlyle's Cromwell (ed. 1), i. 193.

pleasure as I used to read a novel. I have also again taken up my Homer. That is a noble and affecting passage where Diomed and Glaucus, being about to fight, recognize each other as old family friends, exchange arms, and vow to avoid each other henceforth in the fray. (N.B. and this in the tenth year of the war!) After this comes, you know, the meeting of Hector and Andromache, which we read together; altogether a truly Epic canto indeed.

Yet, as I often think, it is not the poetical imagination, but bare Science that every day more and more unrolls a greater Epic than the Iliad; the history of the World, the infinitudes of Space and Time! I never take up a book of Geology or Astronomy but this strikes me. And when we think that Man must go on to discover in the same plodding way, one fancies that the Poet of to-day may as well fold his hands, or turn them to dig and delve, considering how soon the march of discovery will distance all his imaginations, [and] dissolve the language in which they are uttered. Martial, as you say, lives now, after two thousand years; a space that seems long to us whose lives are so brief; but a moment, the twinkling of an eye, if compared (not to Eternity alone) but to the ages which it is now known the world must have existed, and (unless for some external violence) must continue to exist. Lyell in his book about America, says that the falls of Niagara, if (as seems certain) they have worked their way back southwards for seven miles, must have taken over 35,000 years to do so, at the rate of something over a foot a year! Sometimes they fall back on a stratum that crumbles away from behind them more easily : but then again they have to roll over rock that yields to them scarcely more perceptibly than the anvil to the serpent. And those very soft strata which the Cataract now erodes contain evidences of a race of animals, and of the action of seas washing over them, long before Niagara came to have a distinct current ; and the rocks were compounded ages and ages before those strata! So that, as Lyell says, the Geologist looking at Niagara forgets even the roar of its waters in the contemplation of the awful processes of time that it suggests. It is not only that this vision of Time must wither the Poet's hope of immortality ; but it is in itself more wonderful than all the conceptions of Dante and Milton.

To John Allen.

Boulge, Woodbridge,
March 2/48.

My dear Allen,

. . . Every year I have less and less desire to go to London : and now you are not there I have one reason the less for going there. I want to settle myself in some town—for good—for life! A pleasant country town, a cathedral town perhaps! What sort of a place is Lichfield ?

I say nothing about French Revolutions, which are too big for a little letter. I think we shall all be in a war before the year; I know not how else the French can keep peace at home but by quarrelling abroad. But 'come what come may.'

My old friend Major Moor died rather suddenly last Saturday : and this next Saturday is to be buried in the Church to which he used to take me when I was a boy. He has not left a better man behind him.

BOULGE, *Friday*.

MY DEAR ALLEN,

. . . I suppose by a '*Minster Pool*' in Lichfield you mean a select coterie of Prebends, Canons, etc. These would never trouble me. I should much prefer the society of the Doctor, the Lawyer (if tolerably honest) and the singing men. I love a small Cathedral town ; and the dignified respectability of the Church potentates is a part of the pleasure. I sometimes think of Salisbury : and have altogether long had an idea of *settling* at forty years old. Perhaps it will be at Woodbridge, after all !

To E. B. Cowell.

DEAR COWELL,

All I have to say about B. B.'s [1] funeral I have

[1] Bernard Barton's.

sent to the Ipswich Journal—very little—with twenty lines of verse added. You know how little I think of my verses. I never wrote more than twenty good ones in my life. These are not worth twopence—but they came into my head, and so I have treated B. B. as he treated so many others. What solemnity there was at the grave was lost when we got into the Meeting : when three or four very dull but good people spoke in a way that would have been ludicrous but that one saw they were in earnest.

At the grave, Mr. Shewell said some few appropriate words ; but he began to *sing* when once he was in the Chapel.

I am not sure but I must now stop here a week more to look over some of Barton's papers. It appears it will be a comfort to Miss B. to do so. Farewell : let me hear any good news of your wife and yourself.

To F. Tennyson.

BOULGE, WOODBRIDGE, *June* 19, 1849.

MY DEAR OLD FREDERIC,

After you left London, I remained there nearly to the end of December ; saw a good deal of Alfred, etc. Since then I have been down here except a fortnight's stay in London, from which I have just returned. I heard Alfred had been seen flying through town to the Lushingtons : but I did not see him. He is said to be still busy about that accursed Princess. By the by, beg, borrow, steal, or buy Keats' Letters and Poems; most wonderful bits of Poems, written off hand at a sitting, most of them: I only wonder that they do not make a noise in the world. By the by again, it is quite necessary *your* poems should be printed; which Moxon, I am sure, would do gladly. Except this book of Keats, we have had *no* poetry lately, I believe; luckily, the ——, ——, ——, etc., are getting older and past the age of conceiving— *wind.* Send your poems over to Alfred to sort and arrange for you: he will do it: and you and he are the only men alive whose poems I want to see in print. By the by, thirdly and lastly, and in total contradiction to the last sentence, I am now helping to edit some letters and poems of—Bernard Barton! Yes: the poor fellow died suddenly of heart disease; leaving his daughter, a noble woman, almost unprovided for: and we are getting up this volume by subscription. If you were in England *you* must subscribe: but as you are not, you need only give us a share in the Great Grimsby Dock instead.

To George Crabbe.[1]

TERRACE HOUSE, RICHMOND,
October 22/49.

MY DEAR GEORGE,

Warren's analysis of my MS. is rather wonderful

[1] Grandson of the poet, afterwards Rector of Merton, near Watton, Norfolk.

to me. Though not wholly correct (as I think, and as I will expound to you one day) it seems to me yet as exact as most of my friends who know me best could draw out from their personal knowledge. Some of his guesses (though partly right) hit upon traits of character I should conceive quite out of all possibility of solution from mere handwriting. I can understand that a man should guess at one's temperament, whether lively or slow ; at one's habit of thought, whether diffuse or logical ; at one's Will, whether strong and direct or feeble and timid. But whether one distrusts men, and yet trusts friends? Half of this is true, at all events. Then I cannot conceive how a man should see in handwriting such *an accident* as whether one knew much of Books or men ; and in this point it is very doubtful if Warren is right. But, take it all in all, his analysis puzzles me much. I have sent it to old Jem Spedding the Wise. You shall have it again.

If my Mother should remain at this place you must one day come and see her and it with me. She would be very glad to receive you. Richmond and all its environs are very beautiful, and very interesting ; haunted by the memory of Princes, Wits, and Beauties.

To F. Tennyson.

BOULGE, WOODBRIDGE,
August 15/50.

MY DEAR FREDERIC,

Let me hear something of you. The last I heard was three months and more ago, when you announced

I was a Godfather. I replied instantly. Since all this, Alfred has got married. Spedding has seen him and his wife at Keswick : and speaks very highly of her. May all turn out well ! Alfred has also published his Elegiacs on A. Hallam : these sell greatly : and will, I fear, raise a host of Elegiac scribblers.

Since I wrote to you, I have been down here, leading a life of my usual vacuity. My garden shows Autumn asters about to flower : chrysanthemums beginning to assert their places in the beds. The corn cutting all round. I have paid no visits except where the Lady of my old Love resides. A week ago Spedding came down into Suffolk : and we all met : very delightfully. I propose being here till October, and then must, I believe, pay John Allen a visit in Shropshire. Sometimes I turn my thoughts to paying you a visit in Florence this winter : but I doubt that would end in nothing. Yet I have several reasons for going : yourself not the least, pray believe. I have begun to nibble at Spanish : at their old Ballads : which are fine things—like *our*, or rather the North Country, old Ballads. I have also bounced through a play of Calderon[1] with the help of a friend —a very fine play of its kind. This Spanish literature is alone of its kind in Europe, I fancy : with some *Arabian* blood in it. It was at one time over-rated perhaps : I think lately it has undergone the natural reaction of undervaluing. But I am not a fit judge perhaps : and after all shall never make much

[1] *El Mágico Prodigioso.* The friend was Professor Cowell.

study of it.

I was in London only for ten days this Spring: and those ten days not in the thick of the season. So I am more than usually deficient in any news. The most pleasurable remembrance I had of my stay in town was the last day I spent there; having a long ramble in the streets with Spedding, looking at Books and Pictures: then a walk with him and Carlyle across the Park to Chelsea, where we dropped that Latter Day Prophet at his house; then getting upon a steamer, smoked down to Westminster: dined at a chop-house by the Bridge: and then went to Astley's: old Spedding being quite as wise about the Horsemanship as about Bacon and Shakespeare. We parted at midnight in Covent Garden: and this whole pleasant day has left a taste on my palate like one of Plato's lighter, easier, and more picturesque dialogues.

When I speak of the Latter Day Prophet, I conclude you have read, or heard of, Carlyle's Pamphlets so designed. People are tired of them and of him: he only foams, snaps, and howls, and no progress, people say: this is almost true: and yet there is vital good in all he has written. Spedding, beside his Bacon labours, which go on with the quietude and certainty of the Solar System, contributes short and delightful bits to the Gentleman's Magazine: which has now turned over a new leaf, and is really the best Magazine we have. No pert Criticism; but laborious and unaffected information.

Merivale is married! to a daughter of George Frere's, a lawyer in London. I have not heard of M. since this fatal event: but I stayed two days with him in his Essex parsonage just before it. He is grown very fat—an Archdeacon, if ever there were one —and tries to screw himself down to village teaching, etc. He does all he can, I dare say: but what use is an historical Fellow of a College in a Country parish? It is all against the grain with him, and with his people.

You see Daddy Wordsworth is dead, and there is a huge subscription going on for his monument in Westminster Abbey. I believe he deserves one; but I am against stuffing Westminster Abbey with any one's statue till a hundred years or so have proved whether Posterity is as warm about a Man's Merits as we are. What a vast monument is erected to Cider Phillips—to Gay?—the last of whom I love, but yet would not interfere with the perfect Gothic of the Abbey to stick up his ugly bust in it.

I went to one Opera in London—*Zora*—Rossini's own *re*-version of his Moïse. I stayed about an hour and came away. It was good music, well sung, well acted, but the house was hot! To this complexion do we come at last.

Thackeray goes on with Pendennis: which people think very clever, of course, but rather dull. It is nothing but about selfish London people. Dickens's novel [1] is much like his others. I should be sorry not

[1] David Copperfield.

75

to read it, and not to like it.

Pray let me hear from you soon. How do Grimsby railways get on? Give my love to my Godchild. Why don't you send me your Poems? You really ought to do that. Damn the Daguerrotype.

[Written from Bramford? E. F .G. was staying at this time with the Cowells.]

Direct to BOULGE, WOODBRIDGE.
March 7/50.

MY DEAR OLD FREDERIC,

. . . I saw Alfred in London—pretty well, I thought. He has written songs to be stuck between the cantos of the Princess, none of them of the old champagne flavour, as I think. But I am in a minority about the Princess, I believe. If you print any poems, I especially desire you will transmit them to me. I wish I was with you to consider about these: for though I cannot write poems, you know I consider that I have the old woman's faculty of judging of them: yes, much better than much cleverer and wiser men; I pretend to no Genius, but to Taste: which, according to my aphorism, is the feminine of Genius. . . .

. . . Please to answer me directly. I constantly think of you: and, as I have often sincerely told you, with a kind of love which I feel towards but two or three friends. Are you coming to England? How

---

[1] Diogenes and his Lantern.   [2] Old Lady Lambert.

goes on Grimsby! Doesn't the state of Europe sicken you? Above all, let me have any poems you print: you are now the only man I expect verse from; such gloomy grand stuff as you write.

[BOULGE]. *Decr.* 31/50.

MY DEAR OLD FREDERIC,

...As to Alfred, I have heard of his marriage, etc., from Spedding, who also saw and was much pleased with her indeed. But you know Alfred himself never writes, nor indeed cares a halfpenny about one, though he is very well satisfied to see one when one falls in his way. You will think I have a spite against him for some neglect, when I say this, and say besides that I cannot care for his In Memoriam. Not so, if I know myself: I always thought the same of him, and was just as well satisfied with it as now. His poem I never did greatly affect: nor can I learn to do so: it is full of finest things, but it is monotonous, and has that air of being evolved by a Poetical Machine of the highest order. So it seems to be with him now, at least to me, the Impetus, the Lyrical œstrus, is gone. . . . It is the cursed inactivity (very pleasant to me who am no Hero) of this 19th century which has spoiled Alfred, I mean spoiled him for the great work he ought now to be entering upon; the lovely and noble things he has done must remain. It is dangerous work this prophesying about great Men. . . . I have written enough for to-night : I am now going to sit down and play one of Handel's Overtures as well as I can—Semele, perhaps, a very grand one—then, lighting my lantern, trudge through the mud to Parson Crabbe's. Before I take my pen again to finish this letter the New Year will have dawned—on some of us. 'Thou fool! this night thy soul may be required of thee!' Very well : while it is in this Body I will wish my dear old F. T. a happy New Year. And now to drum out the Old with Handel. Good Night.

New Year's Day, 1851. A happy new Year to you! I sat up with my Parson till the Old Year was past, drinking punch and smoking cigars, for which I endure some headache this morning. Not that we took much ; but a very little punch disagrees with me. Only I would not disappoint my old friend's convivial expectations. He is one of those happy men who has the boy's heart throbbing and trembling under the snows of sixty-five.

To Mrs. Cowell.

60 LINC. INN FIELDS,
Thursday [*Feb.* 1851].

DEAR MRS. COWELL,

It will be a great pleasure to me to do all I can for your poems. I said in my letter to Cowell that I had at home the Volume Fulcher published ; but, as you may have perceived in that little happy visit of yours to Boulge in the Autumn, my Books are not in the best order, and your little Book had slipped timidly away behind some pompous octavos perhaps. I could not find it, though I looked for it several days. Now I think if you can manage to send me that and what MSS. you have directly, I can well take them down into Shropshire with me, and consider them there, as I shall consider the spring flowers there.

It is now just upon a year since I was looking at some of them at Bramford, after my return from Bedford: the spring flowers then coming out in your garden when I used to walk home laden with Keziah's cakes, stopped by a fall of snow at the Hockley's, too late for Mr. Hughes' farewell sermon!

You talk of having all Suffolk about you. I think you should spare me a bit of Bramford. What shall it be? Enclosed with your Poems you shall send either one of Cowell's *slippers*—which I used to wear for him—or a little piece of green ribbon cut into a leaf pattern, which I remember you used to wear this time last year. Yes, send me that, a memorial of the past, and that (elderly knight as I am) I may be encouraged to venture on my critical labours with something like the scarf of fair Lady as a guerdon. This suggestion, begun but half earnestly, really is the one I will abide by in good earnest.

To F. Tennyson.

GOLDINGTON, BEDFORD,
June 8/52.

MY DEAR FREDERIC,

It gave me, as always, the greatest pleasure to hear from you. Your letter found me at my Mother's house, at Ham, close to Richmond; a really lovely place, and neighbourhood, though I say it who am all prejudiced against London and 'all the purtenances thereof.' But the copious woods, green meadows, the Thames and its swans gliding between, and so many villas and cheerful houses and terraced gardens with all their associations of Wits and Courtiers on either side, all this is very delightful. I am not heroic enough for Castles, Battlefields, etc. Strawberry Hill for me! I looked all over it: you know all the pictures, jewels, curiosities, were sold some ten years ago; only bare walls remain: the walls indeed here and there stuck with Gothic woodwork, and the ceilings with Gothic gilding, sometimes painted Gothic to imitate woodwork; much of it therefore in less good taste: all a Toy, but yet the Toy of a very clever man. The rain is coming through the Roofs, and gradually disengaging the confectionary Battlements and Cornices. Do you like Walpole? did you ever read him? Then close by is Hampton Court: with its stately gardens, and fine portraits inside; all very much to my liking. I am quite sure gardens should be formal, and unlike general Nature. I much prefer the old French and Dutch gardens to what are called the English.

I saw scarce any of our friends during the three weeks I passed at Ham. Though I had to run to London several times, I generally ran back as fast as I could; much preferring the fresh air and the fields to the smoke and 'the wilderness of monkeys' in London. Thackeray I saw for ten minutes: he was just in the agony of finishing a Novel: which has arisen out of the Reading necessary for his Lectures, and relates to those Times—of Queen Anne, I mean. He will get £1000 for his Novel. He was wanting to finish it, and rush off to the Continent, I think, to shake off the fumes of it. Old Spedding, that aged and most subtle Serpent, was in his old haunt in Lincoln's Inn Fields, up to any mischief. It was supposed that Alfred was somewhere near Malvern: Carlyle I did not go to see, for I really have nothing to tell him, and I have got tired of hearing him growl: though I do not cease to admire him as much as ever. I also went once to the pit of the Covent Garden Italian Opera, to hear Meyerbeer's Huguenots, of which I had only heard bits on the Pianoforte. But the first Act was so noisy, and ugly, that I came away, unable to wait for the better part, that, I am told, follows. Meyerbeer is a man of Genius: and works up *dramatic* Music: but he has scarce any melody, and is rather grotesque and noisy than really powerful. I think this is the fault of modern music; people cannot believe that Mozart is *powerful* because he is so Beautiful: in the same way as it requires a very practised eye (more than I possess) to recognize the consummate power predominating in the tranquil Beauty of Greek Sculpture. I think Beethoven is rather spasmodically, than sustainedly, grand.

Well, I must take to my third side after all, which I meant to have spared you, partly because of this transparent paper, and my more than usually bad writing. I came down here four days ago: and have this morning sketched for you the enclosed, the common that lies before my Bedroom window, as I pulled up my blind, and opened my shutter upon it, early this morning. I never draw now, never drew well; but this may serve to give a hint of poor old dewy England to you who are, I suppose, beginning to be dried up in the South. W. Browne, my host, tells me that your Grimsby Rail is looking up greatly, and certainly will pay well, sooner or later: which I devoutly hope it may.

I do not think I told you my Father was dead; like poor old Sedley in Thackeray's Vanity Fair, all his Coal schemes at an end. He died in March, after an illness of three weeks, saying 'that engine works well' (meaning one of his Colliery steam engines) as he lay in the stupor of Death. I was in Shropshire at the time, with my old friend Allen; but I went home to Suffolk just to help to lay him in the Grave.

To W. F. Pollock.

BOULGE, WOODBRIDGE,
July 25/53.

MY DEAR POLLOCK,

Thank you for your letter. Though I believed the Calderon to be on the whole well done and entertaining, I began to wish to be told it was so by others, for fear I had made a total mistake : which would have been a bore. And the very free and easy translation lies open to such easy condemnation, unless it be successful.

Your account of Sherborne rouses all the Dowager within me. I shall have to leave this cottage, I believe, and have not yet found a place sufficiently dull to migrate to. Meanwhile to-morrow I am going to one of my great treats : viz. the Assizes at Ipswich : where I shall see little Voltaire Jervis,[1] and old Parke,[2] who I trust will have the gout, he bears it so Christianly.

To T. Carlyle.

BREDFIELD RECTORY, WOODBRIDGE.
August 1, [1855].

DEAR CARLYLE,

I came down here yesterday : and saw my Farming Friends to-day, who are quite ready to do all service for us at any time. They live about two miles

[1] Chief Justice.
[2] Baron Parke, afterwards Lord Wensleydale.

nearer Woodbridge than this place I write from and I am certain they and their place will suit you very well. I am going to them any day : indeed am always fluctuating between this place and theirs ; and you can come down to me there, or here, any day—(for Crabbe and his Daughter will, they bid me say, be very glad if you will come ; and I engage you shan't be frightened, and that the place shall suit you as well as the Farmer's). I say you can come to either place any day, and without warning if you like ; only in that case I can't go to meet you at Ipswich. Beds, etc., are all ready whether here or at the Farmer's. If you like to give me notice, you can say which place you will come to first : and I will meet you at any time at Ipswich.

I think if you come you had best come as soon as possible, before harvest, and while the Days are long and fine. Why not come directly? while all the Coast is so clear ?

Now as to your mode of going. There are Rail Trains to Ipswich from Shoreditch, at 7 a.m. 11 a.m. and 3 p.m. all of which come to Ipswich in time for Coaches which carry you to Woodbridge ; where, if you arrive unawares, any one will show you the way to Mr. Smith's, of Farlingay Hall, about half a mile from Woodbridge ; or direct you to Parson Crabbe's, at Bredfield, about three miles from Woodbridge. You may take my word (will you?) that you will be very welcome at either or both of these places ; I mean, to the owners as well as myself.

Well, then there is a Steamer every Wednesday and Sunday; which starts from Blackwall at 9 a.m.; to go by which you must be at the Blackwall Railroad Station in Fenchurch Street by half past eight. This Steamer gets to Ipswich at $\frac{1}{2}$ past 5 or 6; probably in time for a Woodbridge Coach, but not certainly. It is a very pleasant sail. The Rail to Ipswich takes three or two and a half hours.

Have I more to say? I can't think of it if I have. Only, dear Mrs. Carlyle, please to let me know what C. is '*To Eat—Drink—and Avoid.*' As I know that his wants are in a small compass, it will be as easy to get what he likes as not, if you will only say. If you like Sunday Steam, it will be quite convenient whether here or at Farlingay. Crabbe only is too glad if one doesn't go to his church.

BREDFIELD, *Sunday.*

Scrap for Scrap! I go tomorrow to stay at Farlingay, where you will find me, or I will find you, as proposed in my last. Do not let it be a burden on you to come now, then, or at all; but, if you come, I think this week will be good in weather as in other respects. You will be at most entire Liberty; with room, garden, and hours, to yourself, whether at Farlingay or here, where you must come for a day or so. Pipes are the order of the house at both places; the Radiator always lighting up after his 5 o'clock dinner, and rather despising me for not always doing so. At both places a capital sunshiny airy Bedroom without any noise. I wish Mrs. C. could come, indeed; but I will not propose this; for though my Farm has good room, my Hostess would fret herself to entertain a Lady suitably, and that I would avoid, especially toward Harvest time. Will Mrs. Carlyle believe this? E. F. G.

P.S. Bring some Books. If you don't find yourself well, or at ease, with us, you have really but to go off without any sort of Ceremony as soon as you like: so don't tie yourself to any time at all. If the weather be fair, I predict you will like a week; and I shall like as much more as you please; leaving you mainly to your own devices all the while.

To George Crabbe.

31 GREAT PORTLAND STREET,
Jan. 1, 1857.

MY DEAR GEORGE,

A good New Year to you! Here I am, and have been for the last Fortnight, *alone:* my Wife having gone to Mr. Gurney's, and afterwards to Geldestone: and I remaining here partly to see through that mortgage with W. Browne which you remember my telling you about. There has been plenty of Bother, but I suppose it will be done, like some other things, for Better or Worse.

I am still in a total Quandary about a Place of

Abode. My Wife has been asking about Norwich, where she heard of nothing except a Furnisht House in The Close, and an Unfurnisht on the Thorpe Road. So if we be in East Anglia now, I think we shall have to go to Lowestoft for a time. I want my wife to learn all she can of Housekeeping, and employ herself in it: I think she is given to Profusion, and her Hand is out of practice, of course.

I shall be down at Geldestone myself in a few days, and then settle where to go for a time. It is not Inclination that keeps me unsettled: but the not seeing my way at all clear; a matter in which I may perhaps know some more reason than you or others who would otherwise be far more competent to judge of any such matter than I am.

I have scarce seen any one here: but put my Eyes quite out over a silly Persian Manuscript by Day, and look into the Pit of a Theatre for an Hour at night when I can see no longer. What a waste of Life if *my* Life ever could be worth living. I am rather weary of it.

Give my kind Remembrances to Barlow and his Lady. Tell him I will gladly accept the arm-chair he promises me: but let it not be a luxurious or ornamental one, but a plain Oak Chair: for I like, and will have, all of the plainest in my House.

Goodbye, my dear George: get well, and help me with your good Counsel. I shall go and see you (probably *solus* however) for a day or two ere long, I hope ; and if we be at Lowestoft or elsewhere near you, come to us at any time and for any length of Time.

P.S. The 'Bloody Warrior'[1] says you and I and he are to go to Dresden this year together. I should like it : but we must see—we must see.

To E. B. Cowell.

31 Gt Portland St. London.
Jan. 22/57.

My dearest Cowell,

...I have now been five weeks alone at my old Lodgings in London where you came this time last year ! My wife in Norfolk. She came up yesterday ; and we have taken Lodgings for two months in the Regent's Park. And I positively stay behind here in the old Place on purpose to write to you in the same condition you knew me in and I you ! I believe there are new Channels fretted in my Cheeks with many unmanly Tears since then, 'remembering the Days that are no more,' in which you two are so mixt up. Well, well ; I have no news to tell you. Public Matters you know I don't meddle with ; and I have seen scarce any Friends even while in London here. Carlyle but once ; Thackeray not once ; Spedding and Donne pretty often. Spedding's first volume of Bacon is out ; some seven hundred pages ; and the Reviews already begin to think it over-

---

[1] W. K. Browne, who was a Captain in the Militia.

commentaried. How interested would you be in it! and from you I should get a good Judgment, which perhaps I can't make for myself. I hear Tennyson goes on with King Arthur; but I have not seen or heard from him for a long long while.

Oddly enough, as I finished the last sentence, Thackeray was announced; he came in looking gray, grand, and good-humoured; and I held up this Letter and told him whom it was written to and he sends his Love! He goes Lecturing all over England; has fifty pounds for each Lecture: and says he is ashamed of the Fortune he is making. But he deserves it.   ...But I believe I shall never see you again; I really do believe that. And my Paper is gradually overcome as I write this: and I must say Good Bye. Good Bye, my dear dear Friends! I dare not meddle with Mr. and Mrs. Charlesworth.[1] Thackeray coming in overset me, with one thing and another. Farewell. Write to me; direct—whither? For till I see better how we get on I dare fix on no place to live or die in. Direct to me at Crabbe's, Bredfield, till you hear further.

24 PORTLAND TERRACE,
REGENT'S PARK.

MY DEAR COWELL,

 . . . March 12. You see I leave this Letter like an unfinished Picture; giving it a touch every

---

[1] Mrs. Cowell's father and mother.

now and then. Meanwhile it lies in a volume of Sir W. Ouseley's Travels. Meanwhile also I keep putting into shape some of that Mantic which however would never do to publish. For this reason ; that anything like a literal Translation would be, I think, unreadable ; and what I have done for amusement is not only so unliteral, but I doubt *unoriental*, in its form and expression, as would destroy the value of the Original without replacing it with anything worth reading of my own. It has amused me however to reduce the Mass into something of an Artistic Shape. There are lots of Passages which—how should I like to talk them over with you ! Shall we ever meet again ? I think not ; or not in such plight, both of us, as will make Meeting what it used to be. Only to-day I have been opening dear old Salámán : the original Copy we bought and began this time three years ago at Oxford ; with all my scratches of Query and Explanation in it, and the Notes from you among the Leaves. How often I think with Sorrow of my many Harshnesses and Impatiences ! which are yet more of manner than Intention. My wife is sick of hearing me sing in a doleful voice the old Glee of 'When shall we Three Meet again ? ' Especially the Stanza, 'Though in foreign Lands we sigh, Parcht beneath a hostile Sky, etc.' How often too I think of the grand Song written by some Scotch Lady,[1] which I sing to myself for you on Ganges Banks !

[1] Evan Banks, by Miss Williams. See Allan Cunningham's Songs of Scotland, iv. 59.

Slow spreads the Gloom my Soul desires,
The Sun from India's Shore retires :
To *Orwell's* Bank, with temperate ray—
Home of my Youth !—he leads the Day :
Oh Banks to me for ever dear,
Oh Stream whose Murmur meets my Ear ;
Oh all my Hopes of Bliss abide
Where Orwell mingles with the Tide.

The Music has come to me for these Words, little
good otherwise than expressive : but there is no use
sending it to India. To India ! It seems to me it
would be easy to get into the first great Ship and
never see Land again till I saw the Mouth of the
Ganges! and there live what remains of my shabby Life.

But there is no good in all such Talk. I never
write to you about Politics in which you know I
little meddle. . . . March 20. Why, see how the
Time goes ! And here has my Letter been lying
in Sir W. Ouseley for the last ten days, I suppose. To-day I have been writing twenty pages
of a metrical Sketch of the Mantic, for such uses
as I told you of. It is an amusement to me to
take what Liberties I like with these Persians, who
(as I think) are not Poets enough to frighten one
from such excursions, and who really do want a
little Art to shape them. I don't speak of Jeláled-
dín whom I know so little of (enough to show
me that he is no great Artist, however), nor of
Hafiz, whose *best* is untranslatable because he is
the best Musician of Words. Old Johnson said
the Poets were the best Preservers of a Language :

for People must go to the Original to relish them.
I am sure that what Tennyson said to you is true :
that Hafiz is the most Eastern—or, he should have
said, most *Persian* — of the Persians.   He is the
best representative of their character, whether his
Sáki and Wine be real or mystical.   Their Religion
and Philosophy is soon seen through, and always
seems to me *cuckooed* over like a borrowed thing,
which people, once having got, don't know how
to parade enough.   To be sure, their Roses and
Nightingales are repeated enough ; but Hafiz and
old Omar Khayyám ring like true Metal.   The
Philosophy of the Latter is, alas !, one that never
fails in the World.   ' To-day is ours, etc.'

                              24 PORTLAND TERRACE,
                                 REGENT'S PARK.
                                    March 29, [1857].

MY DEAR COWELL,

   I only posted my last long letter four days ago :
and how far shall I get with this ?   Like the
other, I keep it in Sir W. Ouseley, and note down
a bit now and then.   When the time for the Mail
comes, the sheet shall go whether full or not.   I
had a letter from your Mother telling me she had
heard from you—all well—but the Heats increasing.   I suppose the Crocuses we see even in these
poor little Gardens hereabout would wither in a
Glance of your Sun.   Now the black Trees in the
Regent's Park opposite are beginning to show green

Buds ; and Men come by with great Baskets of Flowers ; Primroses, Hepaticas, Crocuses, great Daisies, etc., calling as they go, 'Growing, Growing, Growing ! All the Glory going ! ' So my wife says she has heard them call : some old Street cry, no doubt, of which we have so few now remaining. It will almost make you smell them all the way from Calcutta. 'All the Glory going !' What has put me upon beginning with this Sheet so soon is, that, (having done my ·Will for the present with the Mantic — one reason being that I am afraid to meddle more with N. Newton's tender MS., and another reason that I now lay by what I have sketched out so as to happen on it again one day with fresh eyes) — I say, this being shelved, I took up old Hafiz again, and began with him where I left off in November at Brighton. And this morning came to an ode we did together this time two years ago when you were at Spiers' in Oxford. . . . How it brought all back to me ! Oriel opposite, and the Militia in Broad Street, and the old Canary-coloured Sofa and the Cocoa or Tea on the Table ! . . .

Well ; and I have had a Note from Garcin de Tassy whom I had asked if he knew of any Copy of Omar Khayyám in all the Paris Libraries : he writes 'I have made, by means of a Friend, etc.' But I shall enclose his Note to amuse you. Now what I mean to do is, in return for his politeness to me, to copy out as well as I can the Tetrastichs as you copied them for me, and send them as a Present to De Tassy. Perhaps he will edit them. I should not wish him to do so if there were any chance of your ever doing it ; but I don't think you will help on the old Pantheist, and De Tassy really, after what he is doing for the Mantic, deserves to make the acquaintance of this remarkable little Fellow. Indeed I think you will be pleased that I should do this. Now for some more Æschylus. Friday, April 17. I have been for the last five days with my Brother at Twickenham ; during which time I really copied out Omar Khayyam, in a way ! and shall to-day post it as a '*cadeau*' to Garcin de Tassy in return for his Courtesy to me. I am afraid, a bad return : for my MS. is but badly written and it would perhaps more plague than profit an English 'savant' to have such a present made him. But a Frenchman gets over all this very lightly. Garcin de Tassy tells me he has printed four thousand lines of the Mantic. And here is April running away and it will soon be time to post you another Letter ! When I once get into the Country I shall have less to write you about than now ; and that, you see, is not much.

Tuesday, April 21. Yours and your wife's dear good Letters put into my hand as I sit in the sunshine in a little Balcony outside the Windows looking upon the quite green hedge side of the Regent's Park. For Green it is thus early, and

such weather as I never remember before at this
Season. Well, your Letters, I say, were put into
my hand as I was there looking into Æschylus
under an Umbrella, and waiting for Breakfast.
My wife cried a good deal over your wife's Letter,
I think, I think so. Ah me! I would not as yet
read it, for I was already sad; but I shall answer
hers to me which I did read indeed with many
thoughts : perhaps I can write this post; at least
I will clear off this letter to you, my dear Cowell.

E. F. G.

LONDON, May 7/57.

MY DEAR COWELL,

Well, I have not turned over Johnson's Dictionary
for the last month, having got hold of Æschylus. I
think I want to turn his Trilogy into what shall be
readable English Verse; a thing I have always
thought of, but was frightened at the Chorus. So I
am now; I can't think them so fine as People talk
of : they are terribly maimed; and all such Lyrics
require a better Poet than I am to set forth in
English. But the better Poets won't do it; and I
cannot find one readable translation. I shall (if I
make one) make a very free one; not for Scholars,
but for those who are ignorant of Greek, and who (so
far as I have seen) have never been induced to learn
it by any Translations yet made of these Plays. I

think I shall become a bore, of the Bowring order, by all this Translation : but it amuses me without any labour, and I really think I have the faculty of making some things readable which others have hitherto left unreadable. But don't be alarmed with the anticipation of another sudden volume of Translations ; for I only sketch out the matter, then put it away ; and coming on it one day with fresh eyes trim it up with some natural impulse that I think gives a natural air to all. So I have put away the Mantic. When I die, what a farrago of such things will be found ! Enough of such matter. . . .

Friday, June 5 ! What an interval since the last sentence ! And why ? Because I have been moving about nearly ever since till yesterday, and my Letter, thus far written, was packt up in a Box sent down hither, namely, Gorlestone Cliffs, Great Yarmouth. Instead of the Regent's Park, and Regent Street, here before my windows are the Vessels going in and out of this River : and Sailors walking about with fur caps and their brown hands in their Breeches Pockets. Within hail almost lives George Borrow who has lately published, and given me, two new Volumes of Lavengro called 'Romany Rye,' with some excellent things, and some very bad (as I have made bold to write to him—how shall I face him !). You would not like the Book at all, I think. But I must now tell you an odd thing, which will also be a sad thing to you. I left London last Tuesday fortnight for Bedfordshire, meaning to touch at Hertford in passing; but as usual, bungled between two Railroads and got to Bedford, and not to Hertford, on the Tuesday Evening. To that latter place I had wanted to go, as well to see it, as to see N. Newton, who had made one or two bungled efforts to see me in London. So, when I got to Bedford, I wrote him a line to say how it was I had missed him. On the very Saturday immediately after, I received a Hertford Paper announcing the sudden Death of N. Newton on the very Tuesday on which I had set out to see him! He had been quite well till the Saturday preceding: had then caught some illness (I suppose some infectious fever) which had been visiting some in his house; died on the Tuesday, and was buried on the Thursday after! What will Austin do without him? He had written to me about your Hafiz saying he had got several subjects for Illustration, and I meant to have had a talk with him on the matter. What should be done? I dare not undertake any great responsibility in meddling in such a matter even if asked to do so, which is not likely to be unless on your part; for I find my taste so very different from the Public that what I think good would probably be very unprofitable.

When in Bedfordshire I put away almost all Books except Omar Khayyám!, which I could not help looking over in a Paddock covered with Buttercups and brushed by a delicious Breeze, while a dainty racing Filly of W. Browne's came startling up to wonder and snuff about me. 'Tempus est quo

Orientis Aurâ mundus renovatur, Quo de fonte
pluviali dulcis Imber reseratur; *Musi-manus* unde-
cumque ramos insuper splendescit; Jesu-spiritusque
Salutaris terram pervagatur.' Which is to be read
as Monkish Latin, like ' Dies Iræ,' etc., retaining the
Italian value of the Vowels, not the Classical. You
will think me a perfectly Aristophanic Old Man when
I tell you how many of Omar I could not help
running into such bad Latin. I should not confide
such follies but to you who won't think them so, and
who will be pleased at least with my still harping
on our old Studies. You would be sorry, too, to
think that Omar breathes a sort of Consolation to
me ! Poor Fellow; I think of him, and Oliver
Basselin, and Anacreon; lighter Shadows among
the Shades, perhaps, over which Lucretius presides
so grimly. Thursday, June 11. Your letter of April
is come to hand, very welcome ; and I am expecting
the MS. Omar which I have written about to London.
And now with respect to your proposed Fraser Paper
on Omar. You see a few lines back I talk of some
lazy Latin Versions of his Tetrastichs, giving one
clumsy example. Now I shall rub up a few more
of those I have sketched in the same manner, in
order to see if you approve, if not of the thing done,
yet of

(*letter breaks off abruptly at the end of the page.*)

June 23. I begin another Letter because I am looking into the Omar MS. you have sent me, and shall perhaps make some notes and enquiries as I go on. I had not intended to do so till I had looked all over and tried to make out what I could of it; since it is both pleasant to oneself to find out for oneself if possible, and also saves trouble to one's friends. But yet it will keep me talking with you as I go along: and if I find I say silly things or clear up difficulties for myself before I close my Letter (which has a month to be open in!) why, I can cancel or amend, so as you will see the whole Process of Blunder. I think this MS. furnishes some opportunities for one's critical faculties, and so is a good exercise for them, if one wanted such! First however I must tell you how much ill poor Crabbe has been: a sort of Paralysis, I suppose, in two little fits, which made him think he was sure to die: but Dr. Beck at present says he may live many years with care. Of this also I shall be able to tell you more before I wind up. The brave old Fellow! he was quite content to depart, and had his Daughter up to give her his Keys, and tell her where the different wines were laid! I must also tell you that Borrow is greatly delighted with your MS. of Omar which I showed him: delighted at the terseness so unusual in Oriental Verse. But his Eyes are apt to cloud: and his wife has been obliged, he tells me, to carry off even the little Omar out of reach of them for a while. . . .

June 27. Geldestone Hall. I brought back my

two Nieces here yesterday : and to-day am sitting as of old in my accustomed Bedroom, looking out on a Landscape which your Eyes would drink. It is said there has not been such a Flush of Verdure for years : and they are making hay on the Lawn before the house, so as one wakes to the tune of the Mower's Scythe-whetting, and with the old Perfume blowing in at open windows. . . .

July 1. June over ! A thing I think of with Omar-like sorrow. And the Roses here are blowing —and going—as abundantly as even in Persia. I am still at Geldestone, and still looking at Omar by an open window which gives over a Greener Landscape than yours. To-morrow my eldest Nephew, Walter Kerrich, whom I first took to school, is to be married in the Bermudas to a young Widow. He has chosen his chosen sister Andalusia's Birthday to be married on ; and so we are to keep that double Festival. . . .

Extract from Letter begun 3 *July,* 1857.

Monday, July 13. This day year was the last I spent with you at Rushmere ! We dined in the Evening at your Uncle's in Ipswich, walking home at night together. The night before (yesterday year) you all went to Mr. Maude's Church, and I was so sorry afterward I had not gone with you too ; for the last time, as your wife said. One of my manifold stupidities, all avenged in a Lump now ! I think I shall close this letter to-morrow: which will be the Anniversary of my departure from Rushmere. I went from you, you know, to old Crabbe's. Is he too to be wiped away by a yet more irrecoverable exile than India? By to-morrow I shall have finisht my first Physiognomy of Omar, whom I decidedly prefer to any Persian I have yet seen, unless perhaps Salámán. . . .

Tuesday, July 14. Here is the Anniversary of our Adieu at Rushmere. And I have been (rather hastily) getting to an end of my first survey of the Calcutta Omar, by way of counterpart to our joint survey of the Ouseley MS. then. I suppose we spoke of it this day year; probably had a final look at it together before I went off, in some Gig, I think, to Crabbe's. We hear rather better Report of him, if the being likely to live a while longer is better. I shall finish my Letter to-day; only leaving it open to add any very particular word. I must repeat I am sure this Calcutta Omar is, in the same proportion with the Ouseley, by as good a hand as the Ouseley: by as good a hand, if not Omar's; which I think you seemed to doubt if it was, in one of your Letters. . . .

Have I previously asked you to observe 486, of which I send a poor Sir W. Jones' sort of Parody which came into my mind walking in the Garden here; where the Rose is blowing as in Persia? And with this poor little Envoy my Letter shall end. I will not stop to make the Verse better.

I long for wine ! oh Sáki of my Soul,
Prepare thy Song and fill the morning Bowl ;
For this first Summer month that brings the Rose
Takes many a Sultan with it as it goes.

To Mrs. Charles Allen.

GELDESTONE HALL, BECCLES.
August 15/57.

MY DEAR MRS. ALLEN,

One should be very much gratified at being re-membered so long with *any* kindness : and how much more gratified with so kind Remembrances as yours ! I may safely say that I too remember you and my Freestone days of five and twenty years ago with a particular regard ; I have been telling my Nieces at the Breakfast Table this morning, after I read your letter, how I remembered you sitting in the ' *School-room*'—too much sheltered with Trees—with a large Watch open before you—your Sister too, with her light hair and China-rose Complexion—too delicate ! —your Father, your Mother, your Brother—of whom (your Brother) I caught a glimpse in London two years ago. And all the *Place* at Freestone—I can walk about it as I lie awake here, and see the very yellow flowers in the fields, and hear that distant sound of explosion in some distant Quarry. The coast at Bosherston one could never forget once seen, even if it had no domestic kindness to frame its Memory in. I might have profited more of those good Days than I did ; but it is not my Talent to take the Tide at its flow ; and so all goes to worse than waste !

But it is ungracious to talk of oneself—except so far as shall answer some points you touch on. It would in many respects be very delightful to me to walk again with you over those old Places ; in other respects sad :—but the pleasure would have the upper hand if one had not again to leave it all and plunge back again. I dare not go to Wales now.

I owe to Tenby the chance acquaintance of another Person who now from that hour remains one of my very best Friends. A Lad—then just 16—whom I met on board the Packet from Bristol : and next morning at the Boarding House—apt then to appear with a little *chalk* on the edge of his Cheek from a touch of the Billiard Table Cue—and now a man of 40— Farmer, Magistrate, Militia Officer — Father of a Family—of more use in a week than I in my Life long. You too have six sons, your Letter tells me. They may do worse than do as well as he I have spoken of, though he too has sown some wild oats, and paid for doing so.

My family consists of some eight Nieces here, whom I have seen, all of them, from their Birth upwards—perfectly good, simple, and well-bred, women and girls ; varying in disposition but all agreed among themselves and to do what they can in a small Sphere. They go about in the Village here with some consolation both for Body and Mind for the Poor, and have no desire for the Opera, nor for the Fine Folks and fine Dresses there. There is however some melancholy in the Blood of some of them—but none that mars any happiness but their own : and that but so slightly as one should expect when there was no Fault, and no Remorse, to embitter it !

You will perhaps be as well entertained with this poor familiar news as any I could tell you. As to public matters, I scarcely meddle with them, and don't know what to think of India except that it is very terrible. I always think a Nation with great Estates is like a Man with them :—more trouble than Profit : I would only have a *Competence* for my Country as for myself. Two of my very dearest Friends went but last year to Calcutta :—he as Professor at the Presidency College there : and now he has to shoulder a musket, I believe, as well as deliver a Lecture. You and yours are safe at home, I am glad to think.

Please to remember me to all whom I have shaken hands with, and make my kind Regards to those of your Party I have not yet seen. I am sure all *would be* as kind to me as others who bear the name of Allen *have been*.

Once more—thank you thank you for *your* kindness ; and believe me yours as ever very truly,

EDWD. FITZGERALD.

To E. B. Cowell.

RUSHMERE, *October* 3/57.

MY DEAR COWELL,

I hope things will not be so black with you and us by the time this Letter reaches you, but you may be amused and glad to have it from me. Not that I have come into Suffolk on any cheerful Errand: I have come to bury dear old Mr. Crabbe! I suppose you have had some Letters of mine telling you of his Illness; Epileptic Fits which came successively and weakened him gradually, and at last put him to his Bed entirely, where he lay some while unable to move himself or to think! They said he might lie so a long time, since he eat and drank with fair Appetite: but suddenly the End came on and after a twelve hours Stupor he died. On Tuesday September 22 he was buried; and I came from Bedfordshire (where I had only arrived two days before) to assist at it. I and Mr. Drew were the only persons invited not of the Family: but there were very many Farmers and Neighbours come to pay respect to the remains of the brave old Man, who was buried, by his own desire, among the poor in the Churchyard in a Grave that he wishes to be no otherwise distinguisht than by a common Head and Footstone. . . .

You may imagine it was melancholy enough to me to revisit the house when He who had made it so warm for me so often lay cold in his Coffin unable to entertain me any more! His little old dark Study (which I called the ' *Cobblery* ') smelt strong of its old Smoke : and the last Cheroot he had tried lay three quarters smoked in its little China Ash-pan. This I have taken as a Relic, as also a little silver Nutmeg Grater which used to give the finishing Touch to many a Glass of good hot Stuff, and also had belonged to the Poet Crabbe. . . .

Last night I had some of your Letters read to me: among them one but yesterday arrived, not very sunshiny in its prospects : but your Brother thinks the Times Newspaper of yesterday somewhat bids us look up. Only, all are trembling for Lucknow, crowded with Helplessness and Innocence ! I am ashamed to think how little I understand of all these things : but have wiser men, and men in Place, understood much more? or, understanding, have they *done* what they should ? . . .

Love to the dear Lady, and may you be now and for time to come safe and well is the Prayer of yours,

E. F. G.

31 PORTLAND STREET, LONDON.
Decr. 8/57.

MY DEAR COWELL,

. . . And now about old Omar. You talked of sending a Paper about him to Fraser and I told you, if you did, I would stop it till I had made my Comments. I suppose you have not had time to do what you proposed, or are you overcome with the Flood of bad Latin I poured upon you? Well: don't be surprised (*vext*, you won't be) if *I* solicit Fraser for room for a few Quatrains in English Verse, however—with only such an Introduction as you and Sprenger give me— very short—so as to leave you to say all that is Scholarly if you will. I hope this is not very Cavalier of me. But in truth I take old Omar rather more as my property than yours: he and I are more akin, are we not? You see all [his] Beauty, but you don't feel *with* him in some respects as I do. I think you would almost feel obliged to leave out the part of Hamlet in representing him to your Audience: for fear of Mischief. Now I do not wish to show Hamlet at his maddest: but mad he must be shown, or he is no Hamlet at all. G. de Tassy eluded all that was dangerous, and all that was characteristic. I think these *free* opinions are less dangerous in an old Mahometan, or an old Roman (like Lucretius) than when they are returned to by those who have lived on happier Food. I don't know what you will say to all this. However I dare say it won't matter whether I do the Paper or not, for I don't believe they'll put it in.

[MERTON RECTORY].
September 3/58.

My DEAR COWELL,

...As to my Omar: I gave it to Parker in January, I think: he saying Fraser was agreeable to take it. Since then I

have heard no more ; so as, I suppose, they don't
care about it : and may be quite right. Had I
thought they would be so long however I would have
copied it out and sent it to you : and I will still do
so from a rough and imperfect Copy I have (though
not now at hand) in case they show no signs of
printing me. My Translation will interest you from
its *Form*, and also in many respects in its *Detail :*
very unliteral as it is. Many Quatrains are mashed
together : and something lost, I doubt, of Omar's
Simplicity, which is so much a Virtue in him. But
there it is, such as it is. I purposely said in the very
short notice I prefixed to the Poem that it was so
short because better Information might be furnished
in another Paper, which I thought *you* would undertake. So it rests. Nor have I meddled with the
Mantic lately : nor does what you say encourage me
to do so. For what I had sketcht out was very
paraphrase indeed. I do not indeed believe that
any readable Account (unless a prose Analysis, for
the History and Curiosity of the Thing) will be
possible, for *me* to do, at least. But I took no great
pleasure in what I had done : and every day get
more and more a sort of Terror at re-opening any
such MS. My ' *Go* ' (such as it was) is *gone*, and it
becomes *Work :* and the Upshot is not worth *working*
for. It was very well when it was a Pleasure. So it
is with Calderon. It is well enough to sketch such
things out in warm Blood ; but to finish them in
cold ! I wish I could finish the ' Mighty Magician '

in my new way : which I know you would like, in spite of your caveat for the Gracioso. I have not wholly dropt the two Students, but kept them quite under ; and brought out the religious character of the Piece into stronger Relief. But as I have thrown much, if not into Lyric, into Rhyme, which strikes a more Lyric Chord, I have found it much harder to satisfy myself than with the good old Blank Verse, which I used to manage easily enough. The 'Vida es Sueño' again, though blank Verse, has been difficult to arrange ; here also Clarin is not quenched, but subdued : as is all Rosaura's Story, so as to assist, and not compete with, the main Interest. I really wish I could finish these some lucky day : but, as I said, it is so much easier to leave them alone ; and when I had done my best, I don't know if they are worth the pains, or whether any one (except you) would care for them even if they were worth caring for. So much for my grand Performances : except that I amuse myself with jotting down materials (out of Vocabularies, etc.) for a Vocabulary of *rural* English, or *rustic* English : that is, only the best country words selected from the very many Glossaries, etc., relating chiefly to country matters, but also to things in general : words that carry their own story with them, without needing Derivation or Authority, though both are often to be found. I always say I have heard the Language of Queen Elizabeth's, or King Harry's Court, in the Suffolk Villages : better a great deal than that spoken in London Societies, whether Fashionable or Literary: and the homely [strength] of which has made Shakespeare, Dryden, South, and Swift, what they could not have been without it. But my Vocabulary if ever done will be a very little Affair, if ever done: for here again it is pleasant enough to jot down a word now and then, but not to equip all for the Press.

FARLINGAY, WOODBRIDGE. *Nov.* 2/58.

MY DEAR COWELL,

. . . No. I have not read the Jámí Díwán; partly because I find my Eyes are none the better, and partly because I have now no one to 'prick the sides of my Intent'; not even 'Vaulting Ambition' now. I have got the Seven Castles [1] in my Box here and old Johnson's Dictionary; and these I shall strike a little Fire out of by and by: Jámí also in time perhaps. I have nearly finisht a metrical Paraphrase and Epitome of the Mantic: but you would scarce like it, and who else would? It has amused me to give a 'Bird's Eye' View of the Bird Poem in some sixteen hundred lines. I do not think one could do it as Salámán is done. As to Omar, I hear and see nothing of it in Fraser yet: and so I suppose they don't want it. I told Parker he might find it rather dangerous among his Divines: he took it

[1] Hatifi's Haft Paikar, a poem on the Seven Castles of Bahrám Gúr, as I learn from Professor Cowell, 'each with its princess who lives in it, and tells Bahrám a story.' He adds, 'We always used the name with an understood playful reference to Corporal Trim's unfinished story of the King of Bohemia and *his* Seven Castles.

however, and keeps it. I really think I shall take it back; add some Stanzas which I kept out for fear of being too strong; print fifty copies and give away; one to you, who won't like it neither. Yet it is most ingeniously tesselated into a sort of Epicurean Eclogue in a Persian Garden.

88 Gt. Portland St., London,
Jan. 13/59.

My dear Cowell,

...I am almost ashamed to write to you, so much have I forsaken Persian, and even all good Books of late. There is no one now to 'prick the Sides of my Intent'; Vaulting Ambition having long failed to do so! I took my Omar from Fraser [? Parker], as I saw he didn't care for it; and also I want to enlarge it to near as much again, of such Matter as he would not dare to put in Fraser. If I print it, I shall do the impudence of quoting your Account of Omar, and your Apology for his Freethinking: it is not wholly my Apology, but you introduced him to me, and your excuse extends to that which you have not ventured to quote, and I do. I like your Apology extremely also, allowing its Point of View. I doubt you will repent of ever having showed me the Book. I should like well to have the Lithograph Copy of Omar which you tell of in your Note. My Translation has its merit: but it misses a main one in Omar, which I will leave you to find out. The Latin

Versions, if they were corrected into decent Latin, would be very much better. . . . I have forgotten to write out for you a little Quatrain which Binning found written in Persepolis; the Persian Tourists having the same propensity as English to write their Names and Sentiments on their national Monuments.

GELDESTONE HALL, BECCLES.
April 27 [1859].

MY DEAR COWELL,

Above is the Address you had better direct to in future. I have had a great Loss. W. Browne was fallen upon and half crushed by his horse near three months ago: and though the Doctors kept giving hopes while he lay patiently for two months in a condition no one else could have borne for a Fortnight, at last they could do no more, nor Nature neither: and he sunk. I went to see him before he died — the comely spirited Boy I had known first seven and twenty years ago lying all shattered and Death in his Face and Voice. . . .

Well, this is so: and there is no more to be said about it. It is one of the things that reconcile me to my own stupid Decline of Life—to the crazy state of the world—Well—no more about it.

I sent you poor old Omar who has *his* kind of Consolation for all these Things. I doubt you will regret you ever introduced him to me. And yet you would have me print the original, with many worse things than I have translated. The Bird Epic might be finished at once : but 'cui bono?' No one cares for such things : and there are doubtless so many better things to care about. I hardly know why I print any of these things, which nobody buys ; and I scarce now see the few

To Mrs. Charles Allen.

BATH HOUSE, LOWESTOFT.
October 26 [1859].

DEAR MRS. ALLEN,

I must thank you for your so kind Letter, and kind Invitation. But if I was but five Days with my old College Friend after twelve years' Promise, and then didn't go just on to Teignmouth to see my Sister, and her Family, I must not talk of going elsewhere — even to Prees — where John is always good enough to be asking me : even in a Letter To day received.

By the way, Last Saturday at Norwich while I was gazing into a Shop, a Woman's Voice said, 'How d' ye do, Mr. FitzGerald?' I looked up : a young Woman too, whom (of course) I didn't know. 'You don't remember me, Andalusia Allen that was!' Now Mrs. Day. I had not seen her since '52, a Girl of, I suppose, twelve, playing some Character in a Family Play. John's Letter too tells me of his son going to College.

But Tenby — I don't remember a pleasanter Place. I can now hear the Band on the Steamer as it left the little Pier for Bristol, the Steamer that brought me and the poor Boy now in his Grave to that Boardinghouse. It was such weather as now howls about this Lodging when one of those poor starved Players was drowned on the Sands, and was carried past our Windows after Dinner : I often remember the dull Trot of Men up the windy Street, and our running to the Window, and the dead Head, hair, and Shoulders hurried past. That was Tragedy, poor Fellow, whatever Parts he had played before.

I think you remember me with Kindness because accidentally associated with your old Freestone in those pleasant Days, that also were among the last of your Sister's Life. Her too I can see, with her China-rose complexion : in the Lilac Gown she wore.

I keep on here from Week to week, partly because no other Place offers : but I almost doubt if I shall be here beyond next week. Not in this Lodging anyhow : which is wretchedly 'rafty' and cold ; lets the Rain in when it Rains : and the Dust of the Shore when it drives : as both have been doing by turns all Yesterday and To day. I was cursing all this as I was shivering here by myself last Night : and in the Morning I hear of three Wrecks off the Sands, and indeed meet five shipwreckt Men with a Troop of Sailors as I walk out before Breakfast. Oh Dear!

Please remember me to your 'Gude Man' and believe me yours truly,

E. F. G.

Pray do excuse all this Blotting : my Paper *won't* dry To day.

To W. H. Thompson.

10 MARINE TERRACE, LOWESTOFT.
Nov. 27, 1859.

MY DEAR THOMPSON,

After a Fortnight's Visit to my Sister's (where I caught Cold which flew at once to my Ears, and there hangs) I returned hither, as the nearest Place to go to, and here shall be till Christmas at all Events. I wish to avoid London this winter : and indeed seem almost to have done with it, except for a Day's Business or Sightseeing every now and then. Often should I like to roam about old Cambridge, and hear St. Mary's Chimes at Midnight—but—but! This Place of course is dull enough : but here's the Old Sea (a dirty Dutch one, to be sure) and Sands, and Sailors, a very fine Race of Men, far superior to those in Regent Street. Also the Dutchmen (an ugly set whom I can't help liking for old Neighbours) come over in their broad Bottoms and take in Water at a Creek along the Shore. But I believe the East winds get very fierce after Christmas, when the Sea has cooled down. You won't come here, to be sure : or I should be very glad to smoke a Cigar, and have a Chat : and would take care to have a Fire in your Bedroom this time : a Negligence I was very sorry for in London.

I read, or was told, they wouldn't let old Alfred's Bust into your Trinity. They are right, I think, to let no one in there (as it should be in Westminster Abbey) till a Hundred Years are past; when, after too much Admiration (perhaps) and then a Reaction of undue Dis-esteem, Men have settled into some steady Opinion on the subject : supposing always that the Hero survives so long, which of itself goes so far to decide the Question. No doubt A. T. will do *that.*

To W. F. Pollock.

10 MARINE TERRACE,
LOWESTOFT.
Febr. 23/60.

MY DEAR POLLOCK,

'Me voilà ici' still ! having weathered it out so long. No bad Place, I assure you, though you who are accustomed to Pall Mall, Clubs, etc., wouldn't like it. Mudie finds one out easily : and the London Library too : and altogether I can't complain of not getting such drowsy Books as I want. Hakluyt lasted a long while : then came Captain Cook, whom I hadn't read since I was a Boy, and whom I was very glad to see again. But he soon evaporates in his large Type Quartos. I can hardly manage Emerson Tennent's Ceylon : a very dry Catalogue Raisonnée of the Place. A little Essay of De Quincey's gave me a better Idea of it (as I suppose) in some twenty or thirty pages. Anyhow, I prefer Lowestoft, considering the Snakes, Sand-leaches, Mosquitos, etc. I suppose Russell's Indian Diary is over-coloured : but I feel sure it's true in the Main : and he has the Art to make one feel in the thick of it ; quite enough in the Thick, however. Sir C. Napier came here to try and get the Beachmen to enlist in the Naval Reserve. Not one would go : they won't give up their Independence : and so really half starve here during Winter. Then Spring comes and they go and catch the Herrings which, if left alone, would multiply by Millions by Autumn : and so kill their Golden Goose. They are a strange set of Fellows. I think a Law ought to be made against their Spring Fishing : more important, for their own sakes, than Game Laws.

I laid out half a crown on your Fraser [1] : and liked much of it very much : especially the Beginning about the Advantage the Novelist has over the Play-writer. A little too much always about Miss Austen, whom yet I think quite capital in a Circle I have found quite unendurable to walk in. Thackeray's first Number was famous, I thought : his own little Round about Paper so pleasant : but the Second Number, I

---

[1] Article on ' British Novelists' in Fraser's Magazine, Jan. 1860.

say, lets the Cockney in already : about Hogarth :
Lewes is vulgar : and I don't think one can care
much for Thackeray's Novel. He is always talking
so of himself, too. I have been very glad to find I
could take to a Novel again, in Trollope's Barchester
Towers, etc. : not perfect, like Miss Austen : but
then so much wider Scope : and perfect enough to
make me feel I know the People though caricatured
or carelessly drawn. I doubt if you can read my
writing here : or whether it will be worth your Pains
to do so. If you can, or can not, one Day write me
a Line, which I will read. I suppose when the Fields
and Hedges begin to grow green I shall move a little
further inland to be among them.

To Mrs. Cowell.

FARLINGAY, WOODBRIDGE,
August 21/60.

DEAR MRS. COWELL,

I have been here three months : the house going
on as usual but for the Hostess who has dropt away.
Mr. Smith is very well : and is now in the middle
of Harvest. We have had such a wet Summer as
has not been recollected since 1816, I believe : and
I doubt we have not done with it yet. I go on here
really seeing nobody except the few Farmers and
Farmers' wives connected with the House. I have
been but once to Ipswich in these three months !
when I called on C. E. Cowell, who was out. He
said he should drive over here one day ; but has
not done so yet. Oh yes, I drove through Ipswich
once again with Alfred Smith on our way to his

Tuddenham. . . .

I have never set foot in London since last March year, except running through to Dorsetshire last Autumn : nor have I set eyes on Donne, Spedding, or any of the Wise Men since. It is wrong not to go : but I have lost all Curiosity about what London has to see and hear : its Books come to me here from Mudie : and W. Browne is too much connected with my old Taverns and Streets not to fling a sad shadow over all. As I have not had the courage to go into Bedfordshire, Mrs. B. wished her Boys to come to see me in Suffolk. So I took them to Aldbro', where they were happy Boating and Shooting with a young Sailor, who, strangely enough, reminded me something of their Father as I first knew him near thirty years ago ! This was a strange thing : and my Thoughts run after that poor Fisher Lad who has now gone off in a smack to the North. I always like Seafaring People : and go now every day almost on the Water : either this old Deben here, or on the Sea. Somehow all the Country round is become a Cemetery to me : so many I loved there dead : but none I have loved have been drown'd. Perhaps this poor Sailor who played with W. B.'s Boys as a Boy, and yet took a sort of tender Care of them, will go down into the Deep and blacken that too to my Eyes. . . .   . I have not looked into Persian of late : but I mean if I live to take it up again, and do a little day by day : so as not quite to lose what I have learnt. I do not

119

expect to take any great Interest in it : though I might like the Mesnavi if it were presented to me in a large clear Type.   But I can't give my Eyes up to MSS. for any upshot that Persian is like to render me.   What astonishes me is, Shakespeare : when I look into him it is not a Book, but People talking all round me.   Instead of wearying of him, I only wonder and admire afresh.   Milton seems a Dead-weight compared.

Adieu, both of you.   I don't know where I am to be this Winter : but that is not to be quite here these two Months.   Robert Bloomfield's mother said to him—' Three Giants are coming upon me—Old Age —Winter—Poverty ! '

N.B.   I don't quote this as my case entirely.

To George Crabbe.

MARKET HILL, WOODBRIDGE,
Decr. 28/60.

MY DEAR GEORGE,

. . . I forgot to tell you I really ran to London three weeks ago : by the morning Express, and was too glad to rush back by the Evening Ditto.   I went up for a Business I of course did not accomplish : did not call on, or see, a Friend : couldn't get into the National Gallery : and didn't care a straw for Holman Hunt's Picture.   No doubt, there is Thought and Care in it : but what an outcome of several Years and sold for several Thousands ! What Man with the Elements of a Great Painter

could come out with such a costive Thing after so
long waiting ! Think of the Acres of Canvas Titian
or Reynolds would have covered with grand Outlines
and deep Colours in the Time it has taken to niggle
this Miniature ! The Christ seemed to me only a
wayward Boy : the Jews, Jews no doubt : the Temple
I dare say very correct in its Detail : but think of
even Rembrandt's Woman in Adultery at the National
Gallery ; a much smaller Picture, but how much
vaster in Space and Feeling ! Hunt's Picture stifled
me with its Littleness. I think Ruskin must see
what his System has led to. . .

MARKET-HILL, WOODBRIDGE.
Whit-Monday [*May* 20, 1861]

MY DEAR GEORGE,

. . . I take pleasure in my new little Boat :
and last week went with her to Aldbro' ; and she
' *behaved* ' very well both going and returning ; though,
to be sure, there was not much to try her Temper.
I am so glad of this fine Whit-Monday, when so
many Holiday-makers will enjoy *their*selves, and so
many others make a little money by their Enjoyment.
Our ' Rifles ' are going to march to Grundisburgh,
manuring and *skrimmaging* as they go, and also (as
the Captain [1] hopes) recruiting. He is a right good
little Fellow, I do believe. It is a shame the Gentry
hereabout are so indifferent in the Matter : they

[1] Major Rolla Rouse of Melton.

subscribe next to nothing: and give absolutely nothing in the way of Entertainment or Attention to the Corps. But we are split up into the pettiest possible Squirarchy, who want to make the utmost of their little territory: cut down all the Trees, level all the old Violet Banks, and stop up all the Footways they can. The old pleasant way from Hasketon to Bredfield is now a Desert. I was walking it yesterday and had the pleasure of breaking down and through some Bushes and Hurdles put to block up a fallen Stile. I thought what your Father would have said of it all. And really it is the sad ugliness of our once pleasant Fields that half drives me to the Water where the Power of the Squirarchy stops!

To E. B. Cowell.

MARKET HILL : WOODBRIDGE :
May 22/61.

MY DEAR COWELL,

...My chief Amusement in Life is Boating, on River and Sea. The Country about here is the Cemetery of so many of my oldest Friends: and the petty race of Squires who have succeeded only use the Earth for an *Investment*: cut down every old Tree: level every Violet Bank: and make the old Country of my Youth hideous to me in my Decline. There are fewer Birds to be heard, as fewer Trees for them to resort to. So I get to the Water: where Friends are not buried nor Pathways stopt up: but all is, as the Poets say, as Creation's Dawn beheld. I am happiest going in my little Boat round the Coast to Aldbro', with some Bottled Porter and some Bread and Cheese, and some good rough Soul who works the Boat and chews his Tobacco in peace. An Aldbro' Sailor talking of my Boat said— She go like a Wiolin, she do !' What a pretty Conceit, is it not ? As the Bow slides over the Strings in a liquid Tune. Another man was talking yesterday of a great Storm : ' and, in a moment, all as calm as a Clock.'

By the bye, Forby reasons that our Suffolk third person singular ' It go, etc.,' is probably right as being the old Icelandic form. Why should the 3rd p. sing. be the only one that varies. And in the auxiliaries *May*, *Shall*, *Can*, etc., there *is* no change for the 3rd pers. I incline to the Suffolk because of its avoiding a hiss.

To W. F. Pollock.

MARKET HILL, WOODBRIDGE,
Nov. 20/61.

MY DEAR POLLOCK,

' Vox clamantis ' once again, at something of the usual Season. You have had your Summer Excursions, I suppose : and pray let me hear how you both do after them, and how well prepared to face the Winter. I rather dread it : having, I think, suffered with the Cold last year : and moreover sorry to exchange Boating on the River, in such Glorious

Summer as we have had, for poring one's Eyes out over Mudie's Books at a Sea-coal Fire. Oh, if you were to hear 'Where and oh where is my Soldier Laddie gone' played every three hours in a languid way by the Chimes of Woodbridge Church, wouldn't you wish to hang yourself? On Sundays we have the 'Sicilian Mariner's Hymn'—very slow indeed. I see, however, by a Handbill in the Grocer's Shop that a Man is going to lecture on the Gorilla in a few weeks. So there is something to look forward to.

Donne very kindly came and stayed some days with me: and I think went away looking better than when he arrived. Then Laurence has been painting a Sister of mine: I wouldn't go to look at it for fear of not liking it. He goes on talking of Colour, etc., just as he did twenty years ago—and was about, I believe, to finish my Sister through some '*Amber Medium*' which nobody seemed to wish at all for. (Don't tell Spedding what I say.)

I am extremely pleased with Sainte Beuve's Causeries du Lundi, which I get from the London Library: and try to make the most and longest of its 12 Vols.! Do you know the Book? I suppose it is now almost out of Date in London: but it is as new as 'Soldier Laddie' here.

Fechter's Othello?

To W. H. Thompson.

MARKET HILL, WOODBRIDGE.
Dec. 9/61.

MY DEAR THOMPSON,

The MS. came safe to hand yesterday, thank you : and came out of its Envelope like a Ray of Old Times to my Eyes. I wish I had secured more leaves from that old '*Butcher's Book*' torn up in old Spedding's Rooms in 1842 when the Press went to work with, I think, the Last of old Alfred's Best. But that, I am told, is only a 'Crotchet.' However, had I taken some more of the Pages that went into the Fire, after serving in part for Pipe-lights, I might have enriched others with that which A himself would scarce have grudged, jealous as he is of such sort of Curiosity.

I have seen no more of Tannhäuser than the Athenæum showed me ; and certainly do not want to see more. One wonders that Men of some Genius (as I suppose these are) should so disguise it in Imitation : but, if they be very young men, this is the natural course, is it not ? By and by they may find their own Footing.

As to my own Peccadilloes in Verse, which never pretend to be original, this is the story of *Rubáiyát*. I had translated them partly for Cowell : young Parker asked me some years ago for something for Fraser, and I gave him the less wicked of these to use if he chose. He kept them for two years without using : and as I saw he did'nt want them I printed some copies with Quaritch; and, keeping some for myself, gave him the rest. Cowell, to whom I sent a Copy, was naturally alarmed at it; he being a very religious Man: nor have I given any other Copy but to George Borrow, to whom I had once lent the Persian, and to old Donne when he was down here the other Day, to whom I was showing a Passage in another Book which brought my old Omar up.

(end of letter lost.)

To George Crabbe.

MARKET HILL, WOODBRIDGE,
Jan. 31/62.

DEAR GEORGE,

Thank you always for your Invitations to Merton: why don't I go there? as well as to London, etc. Ah, why! You know, I hope, that you will always be welcome to my seedy home. Board here, Bed at the Bull. But I am (as for the last ten years) looking out for a House, and indeed have gone so far as to have (though without my asking for it) a Plan of Alterations drawn up for a wretched little House (where Mr. Reynolds, once Parson here, used to live), at the end of Seckford Street. But, little as I want, I doubt this would be almost too little, with scarce a Scrap of Garden ground. I had even thoughts of that House where Mr Causton once lived at foot of the Bredfield Sandhill—do you remember? which has a Bit of Garden, and might be altered to my Use. But the House lies low in a Corner where one can't get out except one way—up the hill—and into the Town by those *Ship-meadows*, whereas Seckford Street is high and dry, and leads out to Farlingay, Ipswich Road, etc. But all the better houses are occupied by Dowagers like Myself: the Miss Tolls: Mrs. Pulham: the Miss Silvers: and Billy Whincupp: and none of them will die, or otherwise migrate, for Love or Money: so here I go floundering on and teasing everybody without any Progress at all. I wish you were here, or could give me any Advice from where you are: for I am so certain to blunder in all I do that I quite lose heart to decide. I do really want, however, to get into a house of my own with my own servants (where and with whom, of course, I shan't do half as well as here), and this for several reasons. Do not forget me in case you hear of any likely Housekeeper or Servant, though I can't yet engage the former because I have no house for her to keep. But a good Maidservant I would almost undertake here, paying her instead of Mrs. Berry's doing so: who hires at 1s. a week such a Slut as even I cannot put up with. We are now, I hope, getting rid of the third since I have been here, and I yesterday went to see about another at Hasketon. Also, if when you are at Norwich, you should see any pretty and quaint Furniture, I should be glad to hear of it, and would even go to Norwich if you knew of a Place where such things were in plenty. When I took my Niece to London in November, I went to the Baker Street Bazaar : but spent what Time and Money I had in the new Chinese Department, where I bought a heap of Things which, however, have chiefly gone in Presents. I however like Oriental Things : their quaint shapes, fine Colours, and musky sandal-wood Scents ; and, though I do not so much look at these things individually, yet their Presence in the Room creates a cheerfulness which is good as one grows old, blind, deaf, and dull. A little time in London would soon set one up in such Things : but I don't care to go there, and perhaps it is as well to have to pick up such Things now and then only.

I have not yet hung up my Pictures, which are now got back to the Room they were outed from : but the Truth is they look so much better on the Floor. I have cleaned and put a thick coat of varnish on the Secretary ; this fills up some cracks, though it makes him a little too glossy. Laurence was delighted with my hideous larger Spanish woman, which is certainly Velasquez, he says : I have turpentined her, which (as I have learned from Mr. Churchyard) will freshen up old Varnish, and so do better than overlaying a new Coat of *that*. But what do you think of my Impudence in actually rubbing down my Titian Landscape ! which Mr. C. was frightened to think of my doing, but says it is certainly improved, now it's done. I will not have green skies at any Price. . . .

I should like some of the old light Cane Chairs

such as one used to see in old Inns, Watering Places, etc. Do keep me and my wants of this kind in your Eye, as you have an Eye for such things, and may not be unamused at thus keeping it open.

Here is a stupendous Letter: all about myself. You seem too much engaged, or too little inclined, to write much : and indeed I can't expect other People to repay me with such Coin as my own Idleness can spare so easily. I am reading a Book of almost as dull Letters as my own : the second series of Mrs. Delany : five thick volumes of five hundred pages apiece of almost the poorest twaddle, and often very vulgar Twaddle, from the very greatest People to one another.

To W. H. Thompson.

Good Friday, 1863.

MY DEAR THOMPSON,

Pray never feel ashamed of not answering my Letters so long as you do write twice a year, to let me know you live and thrive. As much oftener as you please : but you are only to be ashamed of not doing that. For that I really want of all who have been very kind and very constant ('*loyal*' is the word that even Emperors now use of themselves) for so many years. This I say in all sincerity.

Now, while you talk of being ashamed of not writing, I am rather ashamed of writing so much

to you. Partly because I really have so little
to say; and also because saying that little too
often puts you to the shame you speak of. You
say my Letters are pleasant, however: and they
will be so far pleasant if they assure you that I
like talking to you in that way: bad as I am at
more direct communication. I can tell you your
letters are very pleasant to me; you at least
have always something to tell of your half-year's
Life: and you tell it so wholesomely, I always say
in so capital a Style, as makes me regret you have
not written some of your better Knowledge for
the Public. I suppose (as I have heard) that your
Lectures [1] are excellent in this way; I can say I
should like very much to attend a course of them,
on the Greek Plays, or on Plato. I dare say you
are right about 'an Apprenticeship in Red Tape
being necessary to make a Man of Business: but
is it too late in Life for you to buckle to and
screw yourself up to condense some of your
Lectures and scholarly Lore into a Book? By
'too late in Life' I mean too late to take Heart
to do it.

I am sure you won't believe that I am *scratching*
you in return for any scratchings from your hands.
We are both too old, too sensible, and too independent, I think, for that sort of thing.

As to my going to Ely in June, I don't know
yet what to say; for I have been Fool enough to

[1] As Greek Professor.

order a Boat to be building which will cost me
£350, and she talks of being launched in the
very first week of June, and I have engaged for
some short trips in her as soon as she is afloat.
I begin to feel tired of her already; I felt I should
when I was persuaded to order her : and that is
the Folly of it. They say it is a very bad Thing
to do Nothing : but I am sure that is not the
case with those who are born to Blunder ; I always
find that I have to repent of what I have done,
not what I have left undone ; and poor W. Browne
used to say it was better even to repent of what
[was] undone than done. You know how glad I
should be if you came here : but I haven't the
Face to ask it, especially after that misfit last
Summer ; which was not my fault however.

I always look upon old Spedding's as one of
the most wasted Lives I know : and he is a wise
Man ! Twenty years ago I told him that he should
knock old Bacon off; I don't mean give him up,
but wind him up at far less sacrifice of Time and
Labour ; and edit Shakespeare. I think it *would*
have been worth his Life to have done those two ;
and I am always persuaded his Bacon would have
been better if done more at a heat. I shall
certainly buy the new Shakespeare you tell me of,
if the Volumes aren't bulky ; which destroys my
pleasure in the use of a Book.

I have had my share of Influenza : even this
Woodbridge, with all its capital Air and self-contented

Stupidity (which you know is very conducive to long Life) has been wheezing and coughing all the very mild winter ; and the Bell of the Tower opposite my Room has been tolling oftener than I ever remember.

Though I can't answer for *June*, I am really meditating a small trip to Wiltshire *before* June ; mainly to see the daughters of my old George Crabbe who are settled at Bradford on Avon, and want very much that I should see how happily they live on very small means indeed. And I must own I am the more tempted to go abroad because there is preparation for a Marriage in my Family (a Niece—but not one of my Norfolk Nieces) which is to be at my Brother's near here ; and there will be a Levée of People, who drop in here, etc. This may blow over, however.

Now I ought to be ashamed of this long Letter : don't you make me so by answering it.

Ever yours, E. F. G.

To Herman Biddell.

MARKET HILL, WOODBRIDGE.
Thursday [1863].

MY DEAR SIR,

Airy first proposed to come this present week : I should have let you know if he had, in hope you would come and meet him here. He now talks of August 10 ; of which you shall hear in time.

As to my going to meet him at your's—beside that you know I may say I go nowhere—(alas! I have not yet found my way to Boulge, where my Brother has been these two months)—I feel it rather indelicate only to break that rule in order to meet an old School-fellow because he happens to be staying at a house where I know I am always kindly invited, and yet don't go. I can tell you truly, that if I went anywhere I should have been much more than once at Playford, where I find sensible, unaffected, and (best of all) unconventional People; and (next best) no formal Dinner: the stupid Dulness of which determined to drive me out of the Society hereabout as much as anything else. However, we must see when Airy does come; he is very obstinate, you know; and makes a rather truculent mouth if one doesn't follow where he bids. You know how I mean all this; he is a real loyal Fellow, as well as a clever; and I am sure I value his old Regard, and like well a Talk of Old Times, and take it very kind that he should give up any holiday, and go to the Expense, for the sake of coming so far to me.

Now, as to Frith, etc., I didn't half read the Review: but sent it to you to see what you would make of it. I quite agree with you about Hogarth, who (I always thought) made his pictures unnatural by overcrowding what was natural in Part, as also by caricature. For this reason, I always thought his Apprentices his best Series. But there are passages of Tragedy and Comedy in his Works that go very deep into Human Nature, and into one's Soul. He was also an Artist in Composition, Colour, etc., though in all respects, I think, a little over-rated of late years.

I don't say that Frith is not more natural (in the sense you use the word, I suppose) than Hogarth; but then does he take so difficult a Face of Nature to deal with, and, even on his own lower ground, does he go to the bottom of it? Is there in his Derby Day the one typical Face and Figure of the Jockey, the Gambler, etc., such as Hogarth would have painted for ever on our Imaginations? Is Frith at all better (if so good) as Leech in Punch? If as good or better, are his Pictures worth a thousandth Part of the Prices given for them? Which, I think, is the Question with the Reviewer. I don't know about his Colour; but I have never heard of it as beyond the usual.

If we take the mere representation of common Nature as the sum total of Art, we must put the modern Everyday life Novel above Shakespeare: for certainly Macbeth and Coriolanus, etc., did not spout Blank Verse, etc. But they dealt in great, deep, and terrible Passions, and Shakespeare has made them live again out of the dead Ashes of History by the force of his Imagination, and by the 'Thoughts that breathe, and Words that burn' that he has put into their Mouths. Nor can I think that Frith's veracious Portraitures of people eating Luncheons at Epsom are to be put in the Scale with Raffaelle's impossible

Idealisation of the Human made Divine.

As you are a sensible Man, I drop 'Mr.' and 'Esq.' in directing to you. I wish others would do so to me.

To W. B. Donne.

MARKET HILL, WOODBRIDGE.
Sat. July 18/63.

MY DEAR DONNE,

. . . I can hardly tell you whether I am much pleased with my new Boat; for I hardly know myself. She is (as I doubted would be from the first) rather awkward in our narrow River; but then she was to be a good Sea-boat; and I don't know but she is; and will be better in all ways when we have got her in proper trim. Yesterday we gave her what they call '*a tuning*' in a rather heavy swell round Orford Ness: and she did well without a reef, etc. But, now all is got, I don't any the more want to go far away by Sea, any more than by Land; having no Curiosity left for other Places, and glad to get back to my own Chair and Bed after three or four Days' Absence. So long as I get on the Sea from time to time, it is much the same to me whether off Aldbro' or Penzance. And I find I can't sleep so well on board as I used to do thirty years ago: and not to get one's Sleep, you know, indisposes one more or less for the Day. However, we talk of Dover, Folkestone,

135

Holland, etc., which will give one's sleeping Talents a *tuning*.

To George Crabbe.

WOODBRIDGE, *August* 4, [1863].

MY DEAR GEORGE,

I have at last done my Holland : you won't be surprised to hear that I did it in two days, and was too glad to rush home on the first pretence, after (as usual) seeing nothing I cared the least about. The Country itself I had seen long before in Dutch Pictures, and between Beccles and Norwich : the Towns I had seen in Picturesque Annuals, Drop Scenes, etc.

But the Pictures—the Pictures—themselves ?

Well, you know how I am sure to mismanage : but you will hardly believe, even of me, that I never saw what was most worth seeing, the Hague Gallery ! But so it was : had I been by myself, I should have gone off directly (after landing at Rotterdam) to that : but Mr. Manby was with me : and he thought best to see about Rotterdam first : which was last Thursday, at whose earliest Dawn we arrived. So we tore about in an open Cab : saw nothing : the Gallery not worth a visit : and at night I was half dead with weariness. Then again on Friday I, by myself, should have started for the Hague : but as Amsterdam was also to be done, we thought best to go there (as furthest) first. So we went : tore about the town in a Cab as before : and I raced through the Museum seeing (I must say) little better than what I have seen over and over again in England. I couldn't admire the Night-watch much : Van der Helst's very good Picture seemed to me to have been cleaned : I thought the Rembrandt Burgomasters worth all the rest put together. But I certainly looked very flimsily at all.

Well, all this done, away we went to the Hague : arriving there just as the Museum closed for that day; next Day (Saturday) it was not to be open at all (I having proposed to wait in case it should), and on Sunday only from 12 to 2. Hearing all this, in Rage and Despair I tore back to Rotterdam : and on Saturday Morning got the Boat out of the muddy Canal in which she lay and tore back down the Maas, etc., so as to reach dear old Bawdsey shortly after Sunday's Sunrise. Oh, my Delight when I heard them call out ' Orford Lights ! ' as the Boat was plunging over the Swell.

All this is very stupid, really wrong : but you are not surprised at it in me. One reason however of my Disgust was, that we (in our Boat) were shut up (as I said) in the Canal, where I couldn't breathe. I begged Mr. Manby to let me take him to an Inn : he would stick to his Ship, he said : and I didn't like to leave him. Then it was Murray who misled me about the Hague Gallery : he knew nothing about its being shut on Saturdays. Then again we neither of us knew a word of Dutch : and I was surprised how little was known of English in return.

But I shall say no more. I think it is the last foreign Travel I shall ever undertake ; unless I should go with you to see the Dresden Madonna : to which there is one less impediment now Holland is not to be gone through. . . . I am the Colour of a Lobster with Sea-faring : and my Eyes smart : so Good-Bye. Let me hear of you. Ever yours E. F.G.

Oh dear !—Rembrandt's Dissection—where and how did I miss that ?

To W. B. Donne.

MARKET HILL, WOODBRIDGE.

October 4/63.

MY DEAR DONNE,

Very rude of me not to have acknowledged your Tauchnitz[1] before : but I have been almost living in my Ship ever since : and I supposed also that you were abroad in Norfolk. I pitied you undergoing those dreadful Oratorios : I never heard one that was not tiresome, and in part ludicrous. Such subjects are scarce fitted for Catgut. Even Magnus Handel —even Messiah. He (Handel) was a good old Pagan at heart, and (till he had to yield to the fashionable Piety of England) stuck to Opera, and

[1] Euripides.

Cantatas, such as Acis and Galatea, Milton's Penseroso, Alexander's Feast, etc., where he could revel and
plunge and frolic without being tied down to Ortho-
doxy. And these are (to my mind) his really great
works : these, and his Coronation Anthems, where
Human Pomp is to be accompanied and illustrated...

To George Crabbe.

MARKET HILL : WOODBRIDGE.
Jan. 12/64.

MY DEAR GEORGE,

. . . Have we exchanged a word about Thackeray
since his Death ? I am quite surprised to see how I
sit moping about him : to be sure, I keep reading his
Books. Oh, the Newcomes are fine ! And now I
have got hold of Pendennis, and seem to like that
much more than when I first read it. I keep hearing him say so much of it; and really think I shall
hear his Step up the Stairs to this Lodging as in old
Charlotte Street thirty years ago. Really, a great
Figure has sunk under Earth.

To E. B. Cowell.

MARKET HILL : WOODBRIDGE.
Jan. 31/64.

MY DEAR COWELL,

I have only Today got your Letter: have been
walking out by myself in the Seckford Almshouse

Garden till 9 p.m. in a sharp Frost—with Orion
stalking over the South before me—(do you know
him in India? I forget) have come in—drunk a glass
of Porter; and am minded to answer you before I
get to Bed. Perhaps the Porter will leave me stranded,
however, before I get to the End of my Letter.

Before this reaches you—probably before I write
it—you will have heard of Thackeray's sudden Death.
It was told me as I was walking alone in those same
Seckford Gardens on Christmas-day Night; by a
Corn-merchant—one George Manby—(do you remember him?) who came on purpose to tell me—
and to wish me in other respects a Happy Christmas.
I have thought little else than of W. M. T. ever
since—what with reading over his Books, and the few
Letters I had kept of his; and thinking over our
five and thirty years' Acquaintance as I sit alone by
my Fire these long Nights. I had seen very little of
him for these last ten years; *nothing* for the last five;
he did not care to write; and people told me he was
become a little spoiled: by London praise, and some
consequent Egotism. But he was a very fine Fellow.
His Books are wonderful: Pendennis; Vanity Fair;
and the Newcomes; to which compared Fielding's
seems to me coarse work. I don't know yet how his
two daughters are left provided for; the Papers say
well. He had built and furnished a fine House at
7 or 8000 £ cost; which is as good a Property for
them to let or sell as any other, I suppose; and the
Copyright of his Books must also be a good Pro-

perty : always supposing he had not encumbered all these by anticipation.

I was not at all well myself for three months; but either the Doctor's Stuff, or the sharp clear weather, or both, have set me up pretty much as I was before. I have nothing to tell, as usual, of People or Places; for I have scarce stirred from this Place since my little Ship was laid up in the middle of October. Donne writes sometimes; I see an article of his about the Antonines advertised in the present Edinburgh; but that you know is out of my Line. His second son, Mowbray, is lately married to a Daughter (I don't know which) of Mrs. Salmon's; widow of a former Rector here, whom your Elizabeth will remember all about, I dare say.

This time ten years I was lodging at Oxford, reading Persian with you. I doubt I shall never do so again; I am too lazy to turn Dictionaries over now; and indeed had some while ceased to expect much to turn up from them. You are quite right, as a Scholar, to work out the Mine; but you admit that nothing is likely to come out of such Value as from the Greek, Latin, and English, which we have ready to our hands. Did I tell you how pleased I had been with Sophocles and Æschylus in my Boat this Summer?

To George Crabbe.

WOODBRIDGE, *March* 20 [1864].

DEAR GEORGE,

I went to London to see Thackeray's House before the Auction cleared all off. To the Auction I did not go. I was much pleased at the Kensington Museum; Crome's Picture really seemed to me to cut over everything there. Then I went to several Dealers, and two Picture Sales; but have come away with two Pictures I don't want, having missed one which I did much want. This was a Portrait of Pope, in so neglected and battered a Condition I thought to be sure I should buy it for £10 at the end of a Sale. But when some People had bid £3 or £4, a voice called out £10; then £20—£30—£40— and so would have gone on, I suppose to any amount, for it was the great Farrer. The Portrait was, I was sure, done from the Man: and I had planned so nicely how I was to cut it down and make oval! I spoke to Farrer, who had bought my Father's Lady Castlemaine (Lely). He said it was now at Narboro'; we will go see it one day, eh? At this last Sale was a great tawdry Lely sold for £200; I said to Farrer I could not believe it to be Lely; and he said No, it was by Lely's Pupil, Mrs. Beale, who did much for him.

Well, I went to my dear Crystal Palace; was all day upon my Legs in the Streets and half the night too; saw countless Silver Teapots!—just the thing!

and ended by buying a Plated Service! Oh, how base! You would have kept me from such Cowardice; as would the poor Captain, whom I kept thinking of as I went about; also, much of W. M. T. Then I bought some perfectly useless Things at the Baker Street Bazaar; in short, have frittered away in Things I don't care for what might have bought something I should have cared for. Ass!

Bence Jones gave me some Prescription to cool my head of Nights; I still wake up in a Bother. He talked to me a good deal of W. M. T., having known him of late years. He thought he had a foible for Great Folks; I wonder if this was really so.

To E. B. Cowell.

MARKET HILL: WOODBRIDGE.
Nov. 11/64.

MY DEAR COWELL,

Let me hear of you whenever you have something to tell of yourself: or indeed whenever you have a few spare minutes, and happen, to think— of me. I don't forget you: and 'out of sight' is not 'out of mind' with you, and three or four more in the World. I hope you see Donne at times: and you must look out for old Spedding, that melancholy Ruin of the 19th Century, with his half-white-washed Bacon. Perhaps you will see another Ruin—the Author of Enoch Arden. Compare that with the Spontaneous *Go* of Palace of

Art, Mort d'Arthur, Gardener's Daughter, Locksley Hall, Will Waterproof, Sleeping Palace, Talking Oak, and indeed, one may say, all the two volumes of 1842. As to Maud, I think it the best Poem, as a whole, after 1842....

To R. C. Trench.

MARKET HILL : WOODBRIDGE.
February 25/65.

MY DEAR LORD,

Edward Cowell's return to England[1] set him and me talking of old Studies together, left off since he went to India. And I took up three sketched out Dramas, two of Calderon,[2] and have licked the two Calderons into some sort of shape of my own, without referring to the Original. One of them goes by this Post to your Grace ; and when I tell you the other is no other than your own 'Life's a Dream,' you won't wonder at my sending the present one on Trial, both done as they are in the same lawless, perhaps impudent, way. I know you would not care who did these things, so long as they were well done ; but one doesn't wish to meddle, and in so free-and-easy a way, with a Great Man's Masterpieces, and utterly fail : especially when two much better men have been before one. One excuse is, that Shelley and Dr. Trench only took parts of these plays, not caring surely —who can ?—for the underplot and buffoonery

[1] In June 1864.   [2] The third was probably the Agamemnon.

144

which stands most in the way of the tragic Dramas. Yet I think it is as a whole, that is, the whole main Story, that these Plays are capital; and therefore I have tried to present that . whole, leaving out the rest, or nearly so ; and altogether the Thing has become so altered one way or another that I am afraid of it now it's done, and only send you one Play (the other indeed is not done printing : neither to be published), which will be enough if it is an absurd Attempt. For the Vida is not so good even, I doubt : dealing more in the Heroics, etc.

I tell Donne he is too partial a Friend ; so is Cowell : Spedding, I think, wouldn't care. So, as you were very kind about the other Plays, and love Calderon (which I doubt argues against me), I send you *my* Magician.

You will not mind if I blunder in addressing you ; in which I steered a middle course between the modes Donne told me ; and so, probably, come to the Ground !

To W. E. Crowfoot.

MARKET HILL, WOODBRIDGE,
April 3 [1865].

I believe I shall send you in some few days the last Print I shall ever dabble in : taken, though not *translated*, from two of Calderon's[1] most famous ones; the Story and Moral of which will interest you a little, and may interest some others also. Edward Cowell's return from India set me on finishing what I had left and put away these nine years; but I print, not to publish, but because I think they will interest a few people.

I suppose you never read that *aggravating* Book, Clarissa Harlowe? Now, with a pair of Scissors, I *could* make that a readable Book; and being a perfectly *original Work of Genius*, I should like to do that Service to my Country before I die. But I should only be abused, and unsold for my pains.

To W. H. Thompson.

LOWESTOFT : *July* 27 [1866].

MY DEAR THOMPSON,

Your welcome Letter was forwarded to me here To day.

...A clerical Brother in law of mine has lost his own whole Fortune in four of these Companies which have gone to smash. Nor his own only. For, having, when he married my Sister, insisted on having half her Income tied to him by Settlement, *that* half lies under Peril from the 'Calls' made upon him as Shareholder.

At Genus Humanum damnat Caligo Futuri.

[1] The Mighty Magician and Such Stuff as Dreams are made of.
[2] The Second Funeral of Napoleon.

146

So I, trusting in my Builder's Honesty, have a Bill sent in about one third bigger than it should be.

All which rather amuses me, on the whole, though I spit out a Word now and then: and indeed am getting a Surveyor to overhaul the Builder: a hopeless Process, I believe all the while.

Meanwhile, I go about in my little Ship, where I do think I have two honest Fellows to deal with. We have just been boarding a Woodbridge Vessel that we met in these Roads, and drinking a Bottle of Blackstrap round with the Crew.

With me just at present is my Brother Peter, for whose Wife (a capital Irishwoman, of the Mrs. O'Dowd Type) my Paper is edged with Black. No one could be a better Husband than he; no one more attentive and anxious during her last Illness, more than a year long; and, now all is over, I never saw him in better Health or Spirits. Men are not inconsolable for elderly Wives; as Sir Walter Scott, who was not given to caustic Aphorisms, observed long ago.

When I was sailing about the Isle of Wight, Dorsetshire, etc., I read my dear old Sophocles again (sometimes omitting the nonsense-verse Choruses) and thought how much I should have liked to have them commented along in one of your Lectures. All that is now over with you: but you will look into the Text now and then. I have now got Munro's Lucretius on board again. Why is it that I never can take up with Horace—so sensible, elegant, agreeable, and sometimes even grand?

To E. B. Cowell.

LOWESTOFT: *August* 19/66.

MY DEAR COWELL,

I don't wish you to think I am in Woodbridge all this while since your Note came. It was forwarded to me here, where I have been since I wrote to you a week ago. The fact is, I had promised to return on finding that the Kerriches were to be here. So, here I am : living on board my little Ship : sometimes taking them out for a Sail : sometimes accompanying them in a walk. In other respects, I am very fond of this Place, which I have known and frequented these forty years ; till the last three years in company with my Sister Kerrich, who has helped to endear it to me. I believe I shall be here, off and on, some while longer ; as my Brother Peter (who has lately lost a capital Wife) is coming to sail about with me. Should I be at Woodbridge for some days I will let you know.

Do you see 'Squire Allenby,' as the folks at Felixtow Ferry call him? If so, ask him why he doesn't sometimes sail here with his ship ; he would like it, I fancy : and everybody seems to like him.

Only yesterday I finished reading the Electra. Before that, Ajax ; which is well worth re-reading too. I am sorry to find I have only Antigone left of

all the precious Seven ; a lucid Constellation indeed !
I suppose I must try Euripides after this ; some few
of his Plays.

This time ten years—a month ago—we were all
lounging about in the hayfield before your Mother's
House at Rushmere. I do not forget these things :
nor cease to remember them with a sincere, sad, and
affectionate interest : the very sincerity of which
prevents me from attempting to recreate them. This
I wish you and yours, who have been so kind to me,
to believe.

I am going to run again to the Coast of Norfolk—
as far as Wells—to wander about Holkham, if the
Weather permit. We have had too much Wind and
Wet to make such excursions agreeable : for, when
one reached the Places by Sea, the Rain prevented
one's going about on Shore to look about. But now
that there has been rather a better look-out of Weather
for the last few Days, and that—

To W. F. Pollock.

MARKET HILL, WOODBRIDGE
[*October* 1866].

MY DEAR POLLOCK,

(You *shall* have a new Pen !)

I suppose your Country Rambles are over, and
that you are got back to the old Shop. Well then,
let me hear of you, do. I can't forget your kindly
Accosting of me in Holborn in the Spring, when
I was after Carpets, etc. Well, I fitted up two rooms

in my new House (there are only three) and got it
ready for a sick Niece, who was there for two months.
But I have not got into it; but go on here: after
living some forty years in lodgings, one is frightened
at a Change: yet it would be better to go. Meanwhile, here I am. For nearly four months I was
living on board my Big Ship. Bed as well as Board.
She was only laid up in her Mud a week ago; and
here am I returned to mine. Laurence called on me
(he was at my Brother's) just before I had bid Adieu
to my Sea-faring; so I didn't see him. Please to
send me Spedding's new Address; he won't, however,
be obliged to you for doing so, I believe; but I must
have the Old Villain out of his Cart twice a Year at
least. I want you to send me your 'Carte de Visite':
you said you would three or four years ago, but you
have not done so. Can't you send me a good one of
Spedding? He wouldn't, for all I could say to him.
I dare say you have several of him: do send me one:
and not the worst: and one of yourself, Do. I have
written to Blakesley for his; as also to tell him that
his Herodotus seems to me the very best Edition of a
Classic that ever came into my hands. I scarce
know why it is that I always get back to Greek—
(and Virgil) — when in my Ship: but so it is.
Sophocles has been a sort of Craze to me this
Summer. (N.B. Don't be frightened. No Trans
lation threatened! All that done with for ever.)
And Herodotus has been delightful. Now, I turn
again to Mudie. Armadale, have you read? Absurd

as it is, so near being very good, I only wish it were a dozen Volumes instead of Two. It is time to read again The Woman in White: a Masterpiece in its way, I do think. I guessed at Annie Thackeray's new Novel[1] in the Cornhill; so much of her Father: so much of Herself: I think she begins to deal rather too much in Reflections; but her Pictures are delightful: her Children the best I ever read.

'Tis now the very witching Time of night, etc. Now could I drink hot—Grog—and so I will. When I was in my Ship I could smoke and drink—Punch, even —but I shall soon have to give up, now I am laid up.

My Paper is in mourning, for my Brother Peter's Wife: a Capital Woman, who died five months ago. He really loved her, was like a Ship without rudder when he lost her, and has in consequence just married his Housekeeper. I believe he has done well.

Now do write to me; and send me your Photograph, as also The Monster's.

To F. Tennyson.

WOODBRIDGE: *Jan.* 29/67.

My dear Frederic,

...The truth is that a solemnly-inaugurated new Edition of all Bacon was not wanted. The Philosophy is surely superseded; not a Wilderness of Speddings can give men a new interest in the Politics and Letters. The Essays will no doubt always be in request, like Shakespeare. But I am perhaps not a proper Judge of these high matters. How should I? who have just, to my great sorrow, finished 'The Woman in White' for the third time, once every last three Winters. I wish Sir Percival Glyde's Death were a little less of the minor Theatre sort; then I would swallow all the rest as a wonderful Caricature, better than so many a sober Portrait. I really think of having a Herring-lugger I am building named 'Marian Halcombe,' the brave Girl in the Story. Yes, a Herring-lugger; which is to pay for the money she costs unless she goes to the Bottom : and which meanwhile amuses me to consult about with my Sea-folks. I go to Lowestoft now and then, by way of salutary Change : and there smoke a Pipe every night with a delightful Chap, who is to be Captain. I have been, up to this time, better than for the last two winters : but feel a Worm in my head now and then, for all that. You will say, only a Maggot. Well; we shall see. When I go to Lowestoft, I take Montaigne with me; very comfortable Company. One of his Consolations for *The Stone* is, that it makes one less unwilling to part with Life. Oh, you think that it didn't need much Wisdom to suggest that? Please yourself, Ma'am. January, just gone! February, only twenty-eight Days : then March with Light till six p.m. : then April with a blush of Green on the Whitethorn hedge : then May, Cuckoos, Nightingales, etc. ; then June, Ship launched, and nothing but Ship till

November, which is only just gone. The Story of our Lives from Year to Year. This is a poor letter: but I won't set The Worm fretting. Let me hear how you are: and don't be two months before you do so.

To W. B. Donne.

WOODBRIDGE: *Febr.* 15 [1867].

MY DEAR DONNE,

...When your letter was put into my hands, I happened to be reading Montaigne, L. III. Ch. 8, De l'Art de Conferer, where at the end he refers to Tacitus; the only Book, he says, he had read consecutively for an hour together for ten years. He does not say very much: but the Remarks of such a Man are worth many Cartloads of German Theory of Character, I think: their Philology I don't meddle with. I know that Cowell has discovered they are all wrong in their Sanskrit. Montaigne never doubts Tacitus' facts: but doubts his Inferences; well, if I were sure of his Facts, I would leave others to draw their Inferences. I mean, if I were Commentator, certainly: and I think if I were Historian too. Nothing is more wonderful to me than seeing such Men as Spedding, Carlyle, and I suppose Froude, straining Fact to Theory as they do, while a scatter-headed Paddy like myself can keep clear. But then so does the Mob of Readers. Well, but I believe in the Vox Populi of two hundred Years: still more, of two thousand. And, whether we be right or wrong, we prevail : so, however much wiser are the Builders of Theory, their Labour is but lost who build : they can't reason away Richard's Hump, nor Cromwell's Ambition, nor Henry's Love of a new Wife, nor Tiberius' beastliness. Of course, they had all their Gleams of Goodness : but we of the Mob, if we have any Theory at all, have that which all Mankind have seen and felt, and know as surely as Day-light ; that Power will tempt and spoil the Best.

Well, but what is all this Lecture to you for ? Why, I think you rather turn to the re-actionary Party about these old Heroes. So I say, however right you may be, leave us, the many-headed, if not the wise-headed, to go our way, only making the Text of Tacitus as clear for us to flounder about in as you can. That, anyhow, must be the first Thing. Something of the manners and customs of the Times we want also : some Lights from other contemporary Authors also : and then, 'Gentlemen, you will now consider your Verdict, and please yourselves.'

To W. F. Pollock.

WOODBRIDGE, *May* 8/67.

MY DEAR POLLOCK,

Unless you are predestined to vote for a German to fill the chair of Sanskrit to be set up at Cambridge, do vote, and get those you can to vote, for Edward

Cowell. What the other Candidates may be, I don't know; I am sure he is fit for the Place; first, because, though I am not a proper Judge of Sanskrit, or any other Scholarship, I believe I am a Judge of the Stuff a Scholar should be made of : and, of all my learned Friends, I have known none of so unmistakeable Metal as Cowell. And, secondly, among the Qualities that so clearly distinguish him, none is more to be trusted than his Reverence and Modesty, which I know would not let him set up for any Office he was not competent to fill : for which very reason he may not profess the Omniscience, or the sublime Theories, which the Germans have dazzled us with : but he will be sure of what he does profess. Beside having studied Oriental Literature these twenty years, he has been for eight years at Calcutta (Professor of English Literature there), where he studied Sanskrit with the native Pundits, etc. He told me, on his return two years ago, that he had been surprised to find how extremely inaccurate the German Scholars were in that direction : that their grand and plausible Theories would not stand Examination : this he told me long before this Cambridge Professorship was talked of. It was Thompson who first told me of the Scheme, and asked if Cowell would stand : I believe Cowell is now with him at Trinity. I repeat that, whatever the other Candidates may be, I am certain Cowell is a fit man ; and if he be so, I should wish him success over a German, even were he not my Friend, but only an Englishman : whose national Good Sense I have more respect for than all the German Æsthetics, etceterorum.

I have nothing to tell you of mine self—only the old Story—Dormouse Existence here all Winter: now boating on the River: and soon about to put to Sea. I have been reading Thackeray's Novels a third time: I am sure that Fielding is common and coarse work in Comparison.

To E. B. Cowell.

'*Scandal*'; LOWESTOFT, *June* 17 [1867].

MY DEAR COWELL,

I wrote to Elizabeth, I think, to congratulate you both on the result of the Election: I have since had your Letter: you will not want me to repeat what, without my ever having written or said, you will know that I feel. I wrote to Thompson on the subject, and have had a very kind Letter from him.

Now you will live at Cambridge among the Learned; but, I repeat, you would rather live among the Ignorant. However, your Path is cut out for you: and, to be sure, it is a more useful and proper one for you than the cool sequestered one which one might like to travel.

I am here in my little Ship—cool and sequestered enough, to be sure—with no Company but my Crew of Two, and my other—Captain of the Lugger now a-building: .a Fellow I never tire of studying—

If he *should* turn out knave, I shall have done with all Faith in my own Judgment : and if he should go to the Bottom of the Sea in the Lugger—I sha'n't cry for the Lugger.

Well, but I have other Company too—Don Quixote—the 4th Part : where those Snobs, the Duke and Duchess—(how vulgar Great Folks then, as now!) make a Fool and Butt of him. Cervantes should have had more respect for his own Creation : but, I suppose, finding that all the Great Snobs could only *laugh* at the earlier part, he thought he had better humour them. This very morning I read the very verses you admired to me twenty years ago—

Ven muerte tan escondida, etc.

They are quoted ironically in Part iv. Lib. vii. Ch. 38.   Ever yours, E. F. G.

WOODBRIDGE : Oct. 12 [1867].

My dear Cowell,

My Ship is still afloat : but I have scarce used her during the last cold weather. I was indeed almost made ill sleeping two nights in that cold Cabin. I may, however, run to Lowestoft and back ; but by the end of next week I suppose she (the Ship) will be laid up in the Mud ; my Men will have eaten the Michaelmas Goose which I always regale them with on shutting up shop ; and I may come home to my Fire here to read 'The Woman in White' and play at Patience :—which (I mean the Game at Cards so called) I now do by myself for an hour or two every night. Perhaps old Montaigne may drop in to chat with and comfort me : but Sophocles, Don Quixote, and Boccaccio—I think I must leave them with their Halo of Sea and Sunshine about them.

To W. F. Pollock.

WOODBRIDGE, *Nov.* 11 [1867].

MY DEAR POLLOCK,

...Are you overrun in London with 'Champagne Charlie is my Name'? A brutal Thing; nearly worthless—the Tune, I mean—but yet not quite—else it would not become so great a Bore. No : I can see, to my Sorrow, that it has some Go—which Mendelssohn had not. But Mozart, Rossini, and Handel had.

I can't help thinking that Opera will have to die for a time : certainly there seems to be no new Blood to keep it alive : and the Old Works of Genius want rest. I have never heard Faust : only Bits—which I suppose were thought the best Bits. They were expressive—musically ingenious, etc.—but the part of Hamlet—the one Divine Soul of Music, Melody— was not there. I think that such a Fuss can be made about it only because there is nothing better.

To W. A. Wright.

MARKET HILL, WOODBRIDGE.

Dec. 11 [1867].

DEAR SIR,

...But I have also another reason for writing to you. Your 'Master' wrote me word the other day, among other things, that you as well as he wished for my own noble works in your Library. I quite understand that this is on the ground of my being a Trinity man. But then one should have done something worthy of ever so little a niche in Trinity Library; and that I do know is not my case. I have several times told the Master what I think, and know, of my small Escapades in print; nice little things, some of them, which may interest a few people (mostly friends, or through friends) for a few years. But I am always a little ashamed of having made my leisure and idleness the means of putting myself forward in print, when really so many much better people keep silent, having other work to do. This is, I know, my sincere feeling on the subject. However, as I think some of the Translations I have done are all I can dare to show, and as it would be making too much fuss to wait for any further asking on the subject, I will send them if you think good one of these days all done up together; the Spanish, at least, which are, I think, all of a size. Will you tell the Master so if you happen to see him and mention the subject?

Allow me to end by writing myself yours sincerely,

EDWARD FITZGERALD.

To Herman Biddell.

WOODBRIDGE, *Decr.* 22/67.

MY DEAR BIDDELL,

It occurs to me that, when I last saw you, you gave me hopes of finding a *Chanticleer* to replace that aged fellow you saw in my Domains. *He* came from Grundisburgh; and surely you spoke of some such Bird flourishing in Grundisburgh still. I will not hold out for the identical plumage—worthy of an Archangel— I only stipulate for one of the sort: such as are seen in old Story books; and on Church-vanes; with a plume of Tail, a lofty Crest and Walk, and a shrill trumpet - note of Challenge: any splendid colours; black and red; black and Gold; white, and red, and Gold! Only so as he be 'gay,' according to old Suffolk speech.

Well, of course you won't trouble yourself about this: only don't *forget* it, next time you ride through Grundisburgh. Or if, in the course of any Ride, you should see any such Bird, catch him up at once upon your Saddle-bow, and bring him to the distressed Widows on my Estate.

Now, I gladly take this opportunity of wishing you and yours a Happy Christmas and New Year. You know you will be welcome here whenever you choose to come.

EDWARD FITZGERALD

To E. B. Cowell.

12 MARINE TERRACE, LOWESTOFT.
Dec. 28 [1867].

MY DEAR COWELL,

...I have come here to wind up accounts for our Herring-lugger : much against us, as the season has been a bad one. My dear Captain, who looks in his Cottage like King Alfred in the Story, was rather saddened by all this, as he had prophesied better things. I tell him that if he is but what I think him —and surely my sixty years of considering men will not so deceive me at last !—I would rather lose money with him than gain it with others. Indeed I never proposed Gain, as you may imagine : but only to have some Interest with this dear Fellow.

To Herman Biddell.

[*Early in* 1868.]

DEAR BIDDELL,

You were very good to have thought of me and my disconsolate Widows. What I shall do with them as Spring advances, I don't know. But I don't like your Cochins and Dorkings, thank you : no, we must wait for an old-fashioned, Æsop-fable fellow. I wrote to my Nephew in Norfolk only last night—I believe I shall have to advertise if it can be decently done.

Then again, I want a *Drake* (three Widows in

this case also !) ; and in this case also I deprive them of their lawful rights till I find an Old-fashioned Drake (have you one ?) nearest akin to the *Wildfowl*—small, grey, and game-like : not your overgrown prize-fowls.

I think it will end in Hens and Ducks quitting my premises if I delay much longer. . .

To E. B. Cowell.

WOODBRIDGE : *March* 1/69.

MY DEAR COWELL,

. . . My Lugger Captain has just left me to go on his Mackerel Voyage to the Western Coast ; and I don't know when I shall see him again. Just after he went, a muffled bell from the Church here began to toll for somebody's death : it sounded like a Bell under the sea. He sat listening to the Hymn played by the Church chimes last evening, and said he could hear it all as if in Lowestoft Church when he was a Boy, ' Jesus our Deliverer ! ' You can't think what a grand, tender, Soul this is, lodged in a suitable carcase.

To W. F. Pollock.

MY DEAR POLLOCK,

. . .I have made three vain attempts at Vol. I. of Browning—did I tell you ? It seems to me an audacious piece of defiance to the Public whom he had found so long blind to his Merits—'Now you have at last come to accept me, I'll ride over you rough-shod.' But A. T. tells me he 'finds greatness' in the work, call it Poem or what you will. And I should say no more, only I remember old Alfred trying to make us worship Bailey's Festus—magnanimous Great Dog! ...

[1869.]

My dear Pollock,

I meant to have thanked you for your first long, and capital, letter, even had it not been followed by that of yesterday. You think to mystify a poor Country man? Well, it is all capital fooling. Do, pray when you have an idle half-hour, send me any such letters. I cannot return them in kind, *you* know as *I* know: I have not the material, nor the Wit to work upon it. That is quite true.

I have not seen Forster's Landor; not caring much for either party. Forster seems to me a genuine Cockney: be-heroing Goldsmith, Landor, etc., *à outrance*. I remember so well his being red-hot in admiration of Coventry Patmore's first Poems: 'By God, they came up to Tennyson's,' etc. Talking of Tennyson, by the way, I had the curiosity to ask Carlyle (in my yearly Letter) what he thought of Browning's Book. I dare say you have heard him talk on the subject. He writes to me: 'I have read —insisted on reading—Browning's Book. It is full of talent, energy, and effort: but actually without *Back-*

bone or basis of Common-sense. I think it among the absurdest books ever written by a gifted Man.'

Such is the opinion of all the men I know, whose opinion is certainly worth as much as the Newspaper Critics. Then why don't some of you step out into the Newspapers and Magazines, and tell the Truth of the Case? Why does not Venables? Stephen? Pollock? I am sure I would if I could: but I have not the faculty. I can only say, 'I do not like you, Doctor Fell,' but there I stop—knowing I'm right. If Browning were half as great as they say, he would himself write to disclaim any approximation to Tennyson. . . .

To Herman Biddell.

WOODBRIDGE,
Guy Faux Day [1869].

DEAR BIDDELL,

I have thought once or twice that Tennyson himself ought to have that illustration of one of his Poems which Thackeray made, and which I gave to you. If you do not set any particular store by it, let us arrange that, and do you take any other you please from the Book you know of. But if you *do* set store by that particular drawing, why, keep it by all means. I have never mentioned it to Tennyson, and do not suppose that *he* would care very much for it. Yet it seems the right thing to do: for he was a great friend of Thackeray's, and admired *the Man*, without (I suppose) having ever read any of his Books through.

I remember his taking up a No. of Pendennis in my Lodging twenty years ago, reading awhile, and then saying—'How *mature* it is!'—perfectly ripe, seasonable, and perfect, a produce of the Man's Wit and Experience of the World.

I am *sure* that Thackeray's drawing must be better than any of *Doré's*—which I have never seen!

To W. F. Pollock.

WOODBRIDGE, *Dec.* 28/69.

MY DEAR POLLOCK,

I really do think it is very good of you to write to me: I am sure it is very pleasant to me.   This I suppose I have said to you before, and perhaps over and over again.   It is all very true.

I went to my old Lowestoft a fortnight ago, and became (whether by Sea Air, Sea Society, or a Doctor) well enough to smoke a pipe, and drink a Glass of Grog again; both which I had resigned for some while, with no good grace.   For I consider these to give me the pleasantest hour of all the twenty-four. I dare not count on this continuing: always afraid of the Cherub who sits up aloft, etc.

The Lugger has managed to pay off all her Debt, and to put £35 in the pocket of her two Owners. This is the first money we have touched on all our Outlay, after three years loss.   More than one ought to expect, you say, on your principle of 'Noblesse oblige,' so far as *I* am concerned. And very true. And, as I did not embark in the business for Profit, I did not expect more. But, as I did not know all the anxiety it would cause me about all these people's lives, I believe I shall now try to back out of it, the more so as my Captain certainly wishes (with all due regard to me) to be sole Master; mainly, I think, for the proper hold it gives him over his Crew, who do not pay the same regard to a fellow-worker as to an Owner. And now that he has got a clear start he may, if he chooses, be sole Owner: though, as I tell him, I will hold on if he still feel he may want some one at the back of the Throne. But to that he answers not.

It has been a season of considerable gain to all concern'd in the Voyage, not because of the Quantity, and still less of the Quality caught: I suppose the high price of Meat, and much other Provision, has raised the price of Herring. But, as a set-off against present gain, there never has been such damage of Ship and Gear; so, if we have paid for what we had, we shall have to pay for what is to be got.

Here is a fine letter of Business for me to write and for you to read !

Well, I returned here on Christmas Eve, to meet a poor fellow who was to spend his Christmas week with me. Instead of which, I find a Letter from him to say he is too ill to come. Then my Landlord and Landlady were both indisposed; so that, with all this, and even the little life of Woodbridge extinct under

closed Shops and falling Snow, I made a very cheerful time of it.

I found the new Idylls on the Lowestoft Bookstall:
but I can get no more interested in them than in any
of their Predecessors: except the old Morte D'Arthur.
That *that* was the finest subject in the whole Legend
is implied, I think, by the Poet himself attacking it
from the first. The Story—the Motive—of the others
does not interest me in itself; nor do I think that
A. T. has touched the right Key in treating of it.
The whole Legend, and its parts, appear to me
scarce fitted to interest any but the child-like
readers of old knightly days whom they were intended
to amuse, I suppose: not, in the main, *very* much
beyond Jack the Giant-killer, etc., and I think such
Stories are best told in the old simple English of
the Romance itself. When elaborated into refined
modern verse, the 'opus' and the 'materia' seem to
me disproportioned. Something in the same way as
Cowper's Miltonic rhythm was quite out of tune with
Homer. I may be quite wrong in all these reasons
for my indifference to these Poems; I only know I
do not like Dr. Fell; and have some considerable—
perhaps more considerable—reliance on my unreason-
ing than on my reasoning affections in such matters.

And while Guinevere, Pelleas, and Co. leave me
quite unconcerned about them, the Lincolnshire
Farmer positively brought tears to my Eyes. There
were Humanity, Truth, and Nature come back again;
the old Brute becoming quite *tragic* in comparison,

just as Justice Shallow does, seen through Shakespeare's Humour.

All this *aesthetic* is as bad as the Herring business So I will shut up Shop at once: wish you and yours a Happy 1870, and hope to remain through it

Yours sincerely,

E. F. G.

To S. Laurence.

WOODBRIDGE: *Jan.* 20/70.

MY DEAR LAURENCE,

. . . My Captain lives at Lowestoft, and is there at present: he also in anxiety about his Wife who was brought to bed the very same day my Landlady died, and (as a letter from him this morning tells me) has a hard time of it. I should certainly like a large Oil-sketch, like Thackeray's, done in your most hasty, and worst, style, to hang up with Thackeray and Tennyson, with whom he shares a certain Grandeur of Soul and Body. As you guess, the colouring is (when the Man is all well) as fine as his form: the finest Saxon type: with that complexion which Montaigne calls 'vif, mâle, et flamboyant'; blue eyes; and strictly auburn hair, that any woman might sigh to possess. He says it is coming off, as it sometimes does from those who are constantly wearing the close hot Sou'westers. We must see what can be done about a Sketch.

EDWARD FITZGERALD

To W. A. Wright.

WOODBRIDGE, *Jan.* 9/70.

DEAR WRIGHT,

I ought to have written to you about the ' Bealings Bells '[1] which I sent. However, you understood from whom they came, and why they came. I don't think people ever troubled themselves to find out the mystery, looking upon it as one of ' the Major's Crotchets.' These he had : but in general was much wiser with them than the Country Squires who smiled at them. I remember his persisting in it to the last that ' his Bells were rung by no human hand '; but he did not repudiate electrical or atmospheric Agency.

I did not desire Tymms to send you a Revise of your Corrections, for I think he is intelligent and careful enough to be trusted in that way.

One Suffolk word has always been an odd mystery to me : ' *Dutfin*,'[2] a cart Bridle — with Blinkers, I think. Can you make anything of it ?

My Landlady seems to me to get weaker, and to shut in gradually. She is now in bed, feeling herself better there. But, when one feels oneself better in Bed !

My Captain has been over with me, and I believe I shall resign the Lugger to him ; he is too honest to say that he does not wish to be whole, sole, and

---

[1] An Account of the Mysterious Ringing of Bells at Great Bealings, Suffolk, in 1834, . . ., by Major Edward Moor, 1841.

[2] Its etymology is a mystery still.

independent Master of her and himself, little as my interference has ever been. The Man is born to be Master, not Man, in any relation of Life, and I have felt I was in my wrong place finding even the ittle I ever thought I found to blame.

To Thomas Woolner.

LOWESTOFT, *Jan.* 30/70.

DEAR SIR,

. . .1 now post you my Sea Words—a work more fitted to my hands; though I also have my fears for this Immortality also. But these words also just amuse People—for the time—and that is all they were meant for.

The Chief Authority quoted is the Man whose Photo I sent you. I should not make free with his Words if I thought he would ever know, or ever care if he did know. But last year, when he and I were smoking together, his Pipe wanting a light, I pulled out (not knowing) a long Printer's Proof of the Words from my Pocket. Before he put it to the candle, to my consternation he began spelling the text, got a little interested, but totally unconscious how much was his own words, or by any possibility reported by me; so that when I said, 'There—there—light your Pipe,' I saw all was safe as the Mail. Last night he was rejoicing in his little Boy's getting into Trowsers; to-day I am to see them; and then we shall walk and see a new little lugger we have bought—like a couple of Fools.

To S. Laurence.

SUFFOLK HOTEL, LOWESTOFT, *August 2/70.*

DEAR LAURENCE,

. . . The Lugger is now preparing in the Harbour beside me; the Captain here, there, and everywhere; with a word for no one but on business; the other side of the Man you saw looking for Birds' Nests; all things in their season. I am sure the Man is fit to be King of a Kingdom as well as of a Lugger. To-day he gives the customary Dinner to his Crew before starting, and my own two men go to it; and I am asked too: but will not spoil the Fun.

I declare, you and I have seen A Man! Have we not? Made in the mould of what Humanity should be, Body and Soul, a poor Fisherman. The proud Fellow had better have kept me for a Partner in some of his responsibilities. But no; he must rule alone, as is right he should too.

I date from the Inn where my Letters are addressed; but I write in the little Ship which I live in. My Nieces are now here; in the town, I mean; and my friend Cowell and his Wife; so I have more company than all the rest of the year. I try to shut my Eyes and Ears against all tidings of this damnable War, seeing that I can do no good to others by distressing myself.

To W. F. Pollock.

BRIDGEWOOD, *Nov.* 1, [1870].

MY DEAR POLLOCK,

I must say that my savageness against France goes no further than wishing that the new and gay part of Paris were battered down; not the poor working part, no, nor any of the People destroyed. But I wish ornamental Paris down, because then I think the French would be kept quiet till they had rebuilt it. For what would France be without a splendid Palace? I should not wish any such Catastrophe, however, if Paris were now as I remember it: with a lot of old historic houses in it, old Gardens, etc., which I am told are now made away with. Only Notre Dame, the Tuileries, and perhaps the beautiful gilt Dome of the Invalides do I care for. They are historical and beautiful too.

But I believe it would be a good thing if the rest of Europe would take possession of France itself, and rule it for better or worse, leaving the French themselves to amuse and enlighten the world by their Books, Plays, Songs, Bon Mots, and all the Arts and Sciences which they are so ingenious in. They can do all things but manage themselves and live at peace with others: and they should themselves be glad to have their volatile Spirits kept in order by the Good Sense and Honesty which other Nations certainly abound in more than themselves.[1]

I see what I think very good remarks about them in old Palmerston's Papers quoted in my Athenæum.[2] He was just the Man they wanted, I think.

WOODBRIDGE, *Dec.* 5/70.

MY DEAR POLLOCK,

. . . Had not Sunday followed Saturday I was a little tempted to run up to hear Cherubini's Medea, which I saw advertised for the Night. But I believe I should feel strange at a Play now : and probably should not have sat the Opera half out. So you have a good Play,[3] and that well acted, at last, on English Boards ! At the old Haymarket, I think : the pleasantest of all the Theatres (for size and Decoration) that I remember ; yes, and for the Listons and Vestrises that I remember there in the days of their Glory. Vestris, in what was called a 'Pamela Hat' with a red feather ; and, again, singing 'Cherry Ripe,' one of the Dozen immortal English Tunes. That was in 'Paul Pry.' Poor Plays they were, to be sure : but the

---

[1] Ten years before, Nov. 2, 1860, FitzGerald wrote to his old friend, the late Mr. W. E. Crowfoot of Beccles : ' I have been reading with interest some French Memoirs towards the end of the last century : when the French were a cheerful, ingenious, witty, trifling people ; they had not yet tasted of the Blood of the Revolution, which really seems to me to have altered their character. The modern French Novels exhibit Vengeance as a moving Virtue : even toward one another : can we suppose they think less well of it towards us ? In this respect they are really the most barbarous People of Europe.

[2] 29 Oct. 1870.   [3] Gilbert's Palace of Truth.

Players were good and handsome, and — oneself
was young — 1822-3 ! There was Macready's Vir-
ginius at old Covent Garden, an event never to be
forgotten. . . .

WOODBRIDGE, *Jan.* 22, [1871].

MY DEAR POLLOCK,

An Artist[1] to whom I have lent my house for
a while has been teaching me 'Spanish Dominoes,'
a very good Game. He, and I, and the Captain
whose Photo I sent you (did I not?) had a grand
bout with it the other day. If I went about in
Company again I think I should do as old Rossini
did, carry a Box of Dominoes, or pack of Cards,
which I think would set Conversation at ease by
giving people something easy to do beside conversing. I say Rossini did this; but I only know
of his doing it once, at Trouville, where F. Hiller
met him, who has published the Conversations they
had together.

To Mrs. Cowell.

WOODBRIDGE, *May* 17 [1871].

MY DEAR LADY,

My little Yacht is—sold ! for a mess of £200.[2]
It was not the money I wanted : nay, I told the man
who came to buy her that he had better buy another
and a bigger which I knew of. But he came from
Town on purpose to buy mine ; and I let her go.

[1] Edwin Edwards.

What will you say to me? And what will E. B. C.? But one main reason for my decision was — these Eyes of mine which will not let me read; and that was nearly all I had to do on board. But I should scarce have thus decided, if Newson[1] had not been offered a much better Berth, which he boggles at accepting; and Jack is engaged to go with the new owner of the Scandal, as he went with me. But his heart was almost up to his eyes when all was settled.

Well, what are we to do now? If I go to Lowestoft this summer, I must put up with the Pleasure-boats there. Do you think *you* will come to join in them? You know I shall be very glad if you should do so; but you also know that I have always advised you to go for your Holidays to some further-off Place, that will make more of a change for you than Lowestoft does. Let me know where you settle on going: and then perhaps, if the Mountain won't come to Mahomet, why Mahomet, etc.

WOODBRIDGE, *July* 4, [1871.]

DEAR MRS. KEMBLE,

It is a shame that one should only have oneself to talk about; and yet that is all I have; so it shall be short. If you will but tell me of yourself, who have read, and seen, and done, so much more, you will find much more matter for your pen, and also for my entertainment.

Well, I have sold my dear little Ship, because I could not employ my Eyes with reading in her Cabin, where I had nothing else to do. I think those Eyes began to get better directly I had written to agree to the Man's proposal. Anyhow, the thing is done; and so now I betake myself to a Boat, whether on this River here, or on the Sea at the Mouth of it.

Books you see I have nothing to say about. The Boy who came to read to me made such blundering Work that I was forced to confine him to a Newspaper, where his Blunders were often as entertaining as the Text which he mistook. We had 'hangarues' in the French Assembly, and, on one occasion, 'iron-clad Laughter from the Extreme Left.' Once again, at the conclusion of the London news, 'Consolations closed at 91, ex Div.'—And so on. You know how illiterate People will jump at a Word they don't know, and twist it in[to] some word they are familiar with. I was telling some of these Blunders to a very quiet Clergyman here some while ago, and he assured me that a poor Woman, reading the Bible to his Mother, read off glibly, 'Stand at a Gate and swallow a Candle.' I believe this was no Joke of his : whether it were or not, here you have it for what you may think it worth. . . .

To W. F. Pollock.

WOODBRIDGE, *Decr.* 9 [1871].

MY DEAR POLLOCK,

...The Tichborne Trial! I gloat over it every night from 8 to 10, my Boy reading it to me with tolerable fluency. His mistakes amuse me sometimes by showing how errors creep into Print under the Compositor's hands. Yesterday the 'face-smiles' of letters were handed in. We have the honour of contributing one witness from a neighbouring Village to confirm the Claimant's *in*dentity, as the Boy reads it: but he tells me that his Father knows of another who *could* swear to the contrary. I have taken no steps to produce that Witness, however.

How the Devil is it that I have run on so long and so saucily to-night, with all this Snow and Cold! And the Prince of Wales perhaps dead. . . .

This is too bad—an end must be put to this. Goodbye.

[*27 Feb.*, 1872.]

DEAR MRS. KEMBLE,

Had I anything pleasant to write to you, or better Eyes to write it with, you would have heard from me before this. An old Story, by way of Apology—to one who wants no such Apology, too. Therefore, true though it be there is enough of it.

I hear from Mowbray Donne that you were at his

Father's Lectures,[1] and looking yourself. So that is all right. Are your Daughters—or one of them—still with you ? I do not think you have been to see the Thanksgiving Procession,[2] for which our Bells are even now ringing—the old Peal which I have known these—sixty years almost—though at that time it reached my Eyes (*sic*) through a Nursery window about two miles off. From that window I remember seeing my Father with another Squire passing over the Lawn with their little pack of Harriers—an almost obliterated Slide of the old Magic Lantern. My Mother used to come up sometimes, and we Children were not much comforted. She was a remarkable woman, as you said in a former letter: and as I constantly believe in outward Beauty as an Index of a Beautiful Soul within, I used sometimes to wonder what feature in her fine face betrayed what was not so good in her Character. I think (as usual) the Lips: there was a twist of Mischief about them now and then, like that in—the Tail of a Cat !—otherwise so smooth and amiable. I think she admired your Mother as much as any one she knew, or had known.

And (I see by the Athenæum) Mr. Chorley is dead,

[1] At the Royal Institution, on 'The Theatre in Shakespeare's Time.' The series consisted of six lectures, which were delivered from 20th January to 24th February, 1872. On 18th February, 1872, Mrs. Kemble wrote : ' My dear old friend Donne is lecturing on Shakespeare, and I have heard him these last two times. He is looking ill and feeble, and I should like to carry him off too, out of the reach of his too many and too heavy cares.'—' Further Records,' ii. 253.

[2] 27th February, 1872, for the recovery of the Prince of Wales.

whom I used to see at your Father's and Sister's houses. Born in 1808 they say : so, one year older than yours truly E. F.G.—who, however, is going to live through another page of Letter-paper. . .

This is a wretched piece of Letter to extort the Answer which you feel bound to give. But I somehow wished to write : and not to write about myself; and so have only left room to say—to repeat—that I am yours ever sincerely

[1872.]

Dear Mrs. Kemble,

I set off with a Letter to you, though I do not very well know how I am to go on with it. But my Reader has been so disturbed by a Mouse in the room that I have dismissed him—9½ p.m.—and he has been reading (so far as he could get on) Hawthorne's Notes of Italian Travel : which interest me very much indeed, as being the Notes of a Man of Genius who will think for himself independently of Murray &c. And then his Account of Rome has made me think of you more than once. We have indeed left off to-night at Radicofani : but, as my Boy is frightened away by the Mouse, I fancy I will write to you before I take my one Pipe—which were better left alone, considering that it gives but half an hour's rather pleasant musing at the expense of a troubled night. Is it not more foolish then to persist in doing this than being frightened at a Mouse? This is not a mere fancy of the Boy—who is not a

Fool, nor a 'Betty,' and is seventeen years old : he inherits his terror from his Mother, he says : positively he has been in a cold Sweat because of this poor little thing in the room : and yet he is the son of a Butcher here. So I sent him home, and write to you instead of hearing him read Hawthorne. He is to bring some poisoned Wheat for the Mouse to-morrow.

Another Book he read me also made me think of you : Harness : whom I remember to have seen once or twice at your Father's years ago. . .

To W. F. Pollock.

[1872.]

MY DEAR POLLOCK,

I went to London at the end of last week, on my way to Sydenham, where my second Brother is staying, whom I had not seen these six years, nor his Wife. . . . On Saturday I went to the Academy, for little else but to see Millais, and to disagree with you about him ! I thought his three Women and his Highlanders brave pictures, which you think also ; but braver than you think them. The Women looked alive : the right Eye so much smaller than the left in the Figure looking at you that I suppose it was so in the original, so that I should have chosen one of the other Sisters for the position. I could not see any analogy between the Picture and Sir Joshua's Graces, except that there were Three. Nor could I think the

Highlanders in the Landscape vulgar ; they seemed to me in character with the Landscape. Both Pictures want tone, which may mean Glazing : wanting which they may last the longer, and sober down of themselves without the danger of cracking by any transparent Colour laid over them.

I scarce looked at anything else, not having much time. Just as I was going out, who should come up to me but Annie Thackeray, who took my hands as really glad to see her Father's old friend. I am sure she was ; and I was taken aback somehow ; and, out of sheer awkwardness, began to tell her that I didn't care for her new Novel ! And then, after she had left her Party to come to me, I ran off ! It is true, I had to be back at Sydenham : but it would have been better to forgo all that : and so I reflected when I had got halfway down Piccadilly : and so ran back, and went into the Academy again : but could not find A. T. She told me she was going to Normandy this week : and I have been so vext with myself that I have written to tell her something of what I have told you. It was very stupid indeed.

[*August* 1872.

My dear Pollock,

Here is the end of the first week in August, when you thought you might be leaving London. But I don't think you will do so for a few days to come. I have had two Visitors with me for the last few days :

one, Frederic Tennyson, who has come to England on private Business, as also for the purpose of introducing an old Gentleman, who is quite deaf, but a Spiritual Medium, who has discovered the original Mystery of the Free Masons, which they have lost, and which they are either to buy of him, or he will publish it to their total Discomfiture. All this old Frederic is as earnest about as a Man, or a Child, can be. He has left his Deaf Medium in London for a time, while he himself goes on his own Business to Grimsby : but he says he may have to convey the Deaf Medium to Ireland, to be introduced to the Masons there.

'D'ailleurs,' Frederic is very well and young, and seemed pleased to talk over old times again. He left me yesterday : and I am now entertaining a poor Lad who is shut up in some London Office all day, and who came down here to get all the Air and Exercise he could from last Saturday till To-morrow, when he goes back to his Desk, poor Fellow.

WOODBRIDGE, *October* 21 [1872].

MY DEAR POLLOCK,

Once more in England you—and once more in Woodbridge I—and once more the Boy with a Tin Can passes under my window as I write, crying—

Baked 'Ta - to's all hot.

Which shows, if there were nothing else to show, that

182

we are got into Winter Quarters. Up to this time, however, we have little of Winter's cold : warm Wet, rather ; not very healthy, I suppose : but better than Snow and Frost to most men's feelings, and to those of the Poor especially.

By this time you have been to see Mr. Irving in King Charles, I predict, and the low Comedian in

April 22, [1873.]

DEAR MRS. KEMBLE,

One last word about what you call my ' Half-invitation ' to Woodbridge. In one sense it is so ; but not in the sense you imagine.

I never do invite any of my oldest Friends to come and see me, am almost distressed at their proposing to do so. If they take me in their way to, or from, elsewhere (as Donne in his Norfolk Circuit) it is another matter.

But I have built a pleasant house just outside the Town, where I never live myself, but keep it mainly for some Nieces who come there for two or three months in the Summer : and, when they are not there, for any Friends who like to come, for the Benefit of fresh Air and Verdure, *plus* the company of their Host. An Artist and his Wife have stayed there for some weeks for the last two years ; and Donne and Valentia were to have come, but that they went abroad instead.

And so, while I should even deprecate a Lady like you coming thus far only for my sake, who ought

rather to go and ask Admission at your Door, I should
be glad if you liked to come to my house for the
double purpose aforesaid.

My Nieces have hitherto come to me from July
to September or October. Since I wrote to you, they
have proposed to come on May 21; though it may
be somewhat later, as suits the health of the Invalid—
who lives on small means with her elder Sister, who
is her Guardian Angel. I am sure that no friend of
mine—and least of all you—would dissent from my
making them my first consideration. I never ask
them in Winter, when I think they are better in a
Town: which Town has, since their Father's Death,
been Lowestoft, where I see them from time to time.
Their other six sisters (one only married) live elsewhere: all loving one another, notwithstanding.

Well: I have told you all I meant by my ' Half-
Invitation.' These N.E. winds are less inviting than
I to these parts; but I and my House would be very
glad to entertain you to our best up to the End of
May, if you really liked to see Woodbridge as well
as yours always truly

WOODBRIDGE, *May* 1, [1873.]

DEAR MRS. KEMBLE,

I am very glad that you will be Photo-
graphed: though not by the Ipswich Man who did
me, there are no doubt many much better in London.

Of course the whole Figure is best, if it can be
artistically arranged. But certainly the safe plan is to

venture as little as possible when an Artist's hand cannot harmonize the Lines and the Lights, as in a Picture. And as the Face is the Chief Object, I say the safest thing is to sit for the Face, neck, and Shoulders only. By this, one not only avoids any conflict about Arms and Hands (which generally disturb the Photo), but also the Lines and Lights of Chair, Table, etc.

For the same reason, I vote for nothing but a plain Background, like a Curtain, or sober-coloured Wall.

I think also that there should be no White in the Dress, which is apt to be too positive for the Face. Nothing nearer White than such material as (I think) Brussels Lace (?) of a yellowish or even dirty hue; of which there may be a Fringe between Dress and Skin. I have advised Men Friends to sit in a—dirty Shirt !

I think a three-quarter face is better than a Full; for one reason, that I ' ink the Sitter feels more at ease looking somewhat away, rather than direct at the luminous Machine. This will suit you, who have a finely turned Head, which is finely placed on Neck and Shoulders. But, as your Eyes are fine also, don't let them be turned too much aside, nor at all downcast : but simply looking as to a Door or Window a little on one side.

Lastly (!) I advise sitting in a lightly clouded Day ; not in a bright Sunlight at all.

You will think that I am preaching my own Photo to you. And it is true that, though I did not sit with any one of these rules in my head ; but just as I got out of a Cab, etc., yet the success of the Thing made me consider afterward why it succeeded ; and I have now read you my Lecture on the Subject. Pray do not forgo your Intention—nay, your Promise, as I regard it—to sit, and send me the result.

To W. F. Pollock.

[1873.]

MY DEAR POLLOCK,

. . . This is Sunday Night : 10 p.m. And what is the Evening Service which I have been listening to ? The 'Eustace Diamonds': which interest me almost as much as Tichborne. I really give the best proof I can of the Interest I take in Trollope's Novels, by constantly breaking out into Argument with the Reader (who never replies) about what is said and done by the People in the several Novels. I say 'No, no ! She must have known she was lying !' 'He couldn't have been such a Fool ! etc.'

September 18/73.

DEAR MRS. KEMBLE,

I have not forgotten you at all, all these months—What a Consolation to you ! But I felt I had nothing to send among the Alps after you : I have been nowhere but for two Days to the Field of Naseby in Northamptonshire, where I went to identify the spot where I dug up the Dead for Carlyle thirty

years ago. I went; saw; made sure; and now—
the Trustees of the Estate won't let us put up the
Memorial stone we proposed to put up; they approve
(we hear) neither of the Stone, nor the Inscription;
both as plain and innocent as a Milestone, says
Carlyle, and indeed much of the same Nature. This
Decision of the foolish Trustees I only had some ten
days ago: posted it to Carlyle who ans ered from
Dumfries; and his Answer shows that he is in full
Vigour, though (as ever since I have known him) he
protests that Travelling has utterly discomfited him,
and he will move no more. But it is very silly of
these Trustees. . . .

[WOODBRIDGE, 1873.]

DEAR MRS. KEMBLE,

. . . .When I was in
Paris in 1830, just before that Revolution, I stopped
one Evening on the Boulevards by the Madeleine
to listen to a Man who was singing to his Barrel-organ.
Several passing 'Blouses' had stopped also: not only
to listen, but to join in the Songs, having bought little
' *Libretti* ' of the words from the Musician. I bought
one too; for, I suppose, the smallest French Coin;
and assisted in the Song which the Man called out
beforehand (as they do Hymns at Church), and of
which I enclose you the poor little Copy. ' *Le Bon
Pasteur*, s'il vous plait '—I suppose the Circumstances:
the 'beau temps,' the pleasant Boulevards, the then

187

so amiable People, all contributed to the effect this Song had upon me; anyhow, it has constantly revisited my memory for these forty-three years; and I was thinking, the other day, touched me more than any of Béranger's most beautiful Things. This, however, may be only one of 'Old Fitz's' Crotchets, as Tennyson and others would call them. . . .

To John Allen.

GRANGE FARM: WOODBRIDGE
Febr: 21/74.

MY DEAR ALLEN,

. . . As to Politics I scarce meddle with them. I have been glad to revert to Don Quixote, which I read easily enough in the Spanish: it is so delightful that I don't grudge looking into a Dictionary for the words I forget. It won't do in English; or *has not done* as yet: the English colloquial is not the Spanish d? It struck me oddly that — of all things in the world! — Sir Thomas Browne's Language might suit.

They now sell at the Railway Stalls Milnes' Life of Keats for half a crown, as well worth the money as any Book. I would send you a Copy if you liked: as I bought three or four to give away.

You may see that I have changed my Address: obliged to leave the Lodging where I had been thirteen years: and to come here to my own house, while another Lodging is getting ready, which I doubt I shall not inhabit, as it will entail Housekeeping on me. But I like to keep my house for my Nieces: it is not my fault they do not make it their home.

To Mrs. Cowell.

'LITTLE GRANGE'
(by Anna Biddell's order—mark!)
[*April* 1874.]

MY DEAR LADY,

. . . . After hearing from half-a-dozen people that they should have no difficulty in finding a Hen and Chicken Daisy, at last Ellen Churchyard has found me one in a Cottager's Garden at Hasketon. It is now in its little Pot outside my house: and is to be sent off in a Box to you as soon as is possible, for your Professor. I will bet 6d. he has found half a dozen just before my poor little innocent reaches him. . . .

LITTLE GRANGE: WOODBRIDGE,
May 2/74.

DEAR MRS. KEMBLE,

My Castle Clock has gone 9 p.m., and I myself am but half an hour home from a Day to Lowestoft. Why I should begin a Letter to you under these circumstances I scarce know. However, I have long been intending to write: nay, actually did write half a Letter which I mislaid. What I wanted to tell you was—and is—that Donne is going on very well : Mowbray thinks he may be pronounced 'recovered.' You may have heard about him from some other hand before this : I know you will be glad to hear it at any time, from any quarter.

This my Castle had been named by me 'Grange Farm,' being formerly a dependency of a more considerable Château on the hill above. But a fine tall Woman, who has been staying two days, ordered me to call it 'Little Grange.' So it must be. She came to meet a little Niece of mine : both Annies : one tall as the other is short : both capital in Head and Heart : I knew they would *fadge* well : so they did : so we all did, waiting on ourselves and on one another. Odd that I have another tip-top Annie on my small list of Acquaintances—Annie Thackeray.

I wonder what Spring is like in America. We have had an April of really 'magnifique' Weather : but here is that vixen May with its N.E. airs. A Nightingale however sings so close to my Bedroom that (the window being open) the Song is almost too loud.

I thought you would come back to Nightingale-land !

Donne is better : and Spedding has at last (I hear) got his load of Bacon off his Shoulders, after carrying it for near Forty years ! Forty years long ! A fortnight ago there was such a delicious bit of his in Notes and Queries,[1] a Comment on some American Comment

[1] 18 April, 1874. Professor Hiram Corson endeavoured to maintain the correctness of the reading of the Folios in Antony and Cleopatra, v. 2. 86–88 :

> 'For his Bounty, .
> There was no winter in 't. An *Anthony* it was,
> That grew the more by reaping.'

Spedding admirably defended Theobald's certain emendation of 'autumn' for 'Anthony.'

on a passage in Antony and Cleopatra, that I recalled my old Sorrow that he had not edited Shakespeare long ago instead of wasting Life in washing his Blackamoor. Perhaps there is time for this yet: but is there the Will?

Pray, Madam, how do you emphasize the line—

> 'After Life's fitful Fever he sleeps well,'

which, by the by, one wonders never to have seen in some Churchyard? . . . .

LOWESTOFT: *June* 2/74.

DEAR MRS. KEMBLE,

Many a time have I written to you from this place: which may be the reason why I write again now—the very day your Letter reaches me—for I don't know that I have much to say, nor anything worth forcing from you the Answer that you will write. Let me look at your Letter again. Yes: so I thought of '*he* sleeps well,' and yet I do not remember to have heard it so read. (I never heard you read the Play) I don't think Macready read it so. I liked his Macbeth, I must say: only he would say 'Amen st-u-u-u-ck in his throat,' which was not only a blunder, but a vulgar blunder, I think. . . .

Donne—Archdeacon Groome told me a Fortnight ago that he had been at Weymouth Street. Donne better, but still not his former Self.

By the by, I have got a Skeleton of my own at last: Bronchitis—which came on me a month ago—

which I let go on for near three weeks—then was forced to call in a Doctor to subdue, who kept me a week indoors. And now I am told that, every Cold I catch, my Skeleton is to come out, etc. Every N.E. wind that blows, etc. I had not been shut up indoors for some fifty-five years—since Measles at school—but I had green before my Windows, and Don Quixote for Company within. *Que voulez-vous?*

Shakespeare again. A Doctor Whalley, who wrote a Tragedy for Mrs. Siddons (which she declined), proposed to her that she should read—'But screw your Courage to the *sticking* place,' with the appropriate action of using the Dagger. I think Mrs. Siddons good-naturedly admits there may be something in the suggestion. One reads this in the last memoir of Madame Piozzi, edited by Mr. Hayward.

Blackbird v. *Nightingale*. I have always loved the first best: as being so jolly, and the Note so proper from that golden Bill of his. But one does not like to go against received opinion. Your *Oriole* has been seen in these parts by old—very old—people: at least, a gay bird so named. But no one ever pretends to see him now.

Now have you perversely crossed the Address which you desire me to abide by: and I can't be sure of your 'Branchtown'? But I suppose that enough is clear to make my Letter reach you if it once gets across the Atlantic. And now this uncertainty about your writing recalls to me—very absurdly—an absurd Story told me by a pious, but humorous, man, which will please you if you don't know it already.

Scene.—Country Church on Winter's Evening. Congregation, with the Old Hundredth ready for the Parson to give out some Dismissal Words.

Good old Parson, not at all meaning rhyme, ' The Light has grown so very dim, I scarce can see to read the Hymn.'

Congregation, taking it up : to the first half of the Old Hundredth—

> ' The Light has grown so very dim,
> I scarce can see to read the Hymn.'

(Pause, as usual : *Parson,* mildly impatient) ' I did not mean to read a Hymn ; I only meant my Eyes were dim.'

Congregation, to second part of Old Hundredth :—

> ' I did not mean to read a Hymn ;
> I only meant my Eyes were dim.'

Parson, out of Patience, etc. :—

> ' I didn't mean a Hymn at all,—
> I think the Devil's in you all.'

I say, if you don't know this, it is worth your knowing, and making known over the whole Continent of America, North and South. And I am your trusty and affectionate old Beadsman (left rather deaf with that blessed Bronchitis)

To T. Carlyle.

LITTLE GRANGE, WOODBRIDGE,
June 23 [1874].

MY DEAR CARLYLE,

I should certainly write oftener to hear about you if my doing so did not trouble you to dictate an answer. Also, I hear of you from time to time from Pollock; but not lately from him at all: I suppose, busy at this time of London life. So I will write you a little bit: and you can just let me know how you are.

This time last year I was preparing to go to Naseby on that fruitless errand; and last Night I dreamt of you: which may be the immediate cause of my now writing. I thought you were sitting in some room, and you would insist on how much more white-headed you were than I seemed to see you: and you were very kind, and even affectionate; but I said, 'You know you often call me a d——d fool, now, don't you?' and then somehow Spedding laughed from a corner of the room.

What an Old Woman's Dream to write to Thomas Carlyle! Yesterday I met a Lady, not rich, who told me she had bought your French Revolution from money she saved by making her own Dress. Perhaps it was that which made me dream, which makes me write.

I am really thinking of going by sea to Edinburgh, after thinking of so doing for half my Life. You will scarce think my reason for wishing to go is Sir Walter, whom you bid us, look on as no Hero : but who needs will be so to me. So I want to see the Places he wrote about, and the Place he himself lived in.

Last Sunday Evening—the longest day—I was looking at an Elm which you may remember in the field before Farlingay. I remember your reading under it—reading up Voltaire, etc., for Frederick. I thought how big the Tree had grown since that : but that is nineteen years ago, 1855. I have been obliged to leave my Market Hill Lodgings, and come down to the House I built and no one would live in. You would like it, I think, but you would never come : and now some Nieces *are* coming for a Summer Visit : and so I think of getting abroad a little, so as to leave them the house clear.

This really must be a comical Letter. I dare not read it over : but you can but call me what I dreamed you did ; and you will not be sorry that I do wish to hear of you, and that I am still as ever your faithful   E. F. G.

LITTLE GRANGE, WOODBRIDGE,
July 31 [1874].

DEAR MASTER,

You bid me write and tell you if I got to Edinburgh at last. So I have to tell you I did—and much you will care to hear about it ! But I went—by Sea : well pleased with the Coast ; thinking of you at Dunbar, and (I must own) of Sir Walter when they pointed out to me the range of Lammermuir; and of Burns when I saw the Berwick Law by which the Ship rode when the Trooper called for a Pint of Wine in a Silver Tassie to pledge his bonny Mary, before going to the Wars. And Edinburgh looked really beautiful to me that long Evening: and the next day, though I only drove about it, and went into none of the Buildings, not even up the Castle steep, all which looked so grand from my Inn in Princes Street. And (in spite of you) I worshipped at the Scott Monument: and went to Abbotsford next day: glad to find it was not at all the Cockney Castle I had been told of, but a substantial house in the Style common to the Country: with broad walks before, and then a meadow: and then the Tweed: and then the Woods my Hero planted, and which I wished he could see thriving so well. Then Dryburgh—for his sake too; you know. And I was really going home the next day: but had to wait for some money: and was persuaded to take a Cook's passport to Stirling, Katrine, Lomond, etc., which somehow I did not care for: and on the fourth day back to London by Rail. And, after a visit to my old Brother Peter, and my old friend Donne there, back here. A long way to go for so little purpose, you may think — my little Pilgrimage to my Mecca!

The Country about Edinburgh reminded me of Dublin, only not so green; the City beautiful. I should not be sorry to go again; but I suppose never shall.

So here is the upshot of my long-proposed Pilgrimage. I was told in London that you were gone North: if this Letter (written to order) should follow you, pray do not trouble yourself to acknowledge it, but believe me your heretical Hero-worshipper

E. F. G.

Now for a Pipe in my Garden—to think over all these little things.

LOWESTOFT, *Feb*. 11/75.

DEAR MRS. KEMBLE,

...Your Photograph—Yes—I saw your Mother in it, as I saw her in you when you came to us in Woodbridge in 1852. That is, I saw her such as I had seen her in a little sixpenny Engraving in a 'Cottage Bonnet,' something such as you wore when you stept out of your Chaise at the Crown Inn.

My Mother always said that your Mother was by far the most witty, sensible, and agreeable Woman she knew. I remember one of the very few delightful Dinner parties I ever was at—in St. James' Place—(was it?) a Party of seven or eight, at a round Table, your Mother at the head of the Table, and Mrs. F. Kemble my next Neighbour. And really the (almost) only other pleasant Dinner was one you gave me and the Donnes in Savile Row, before going to see Wigan in 'Still Waters,' which you said was *your* Play, in so far as you had suggested the Story from some French Novel.

I used to think what a deep current of melancholy was under your Mother's Humour. Not 'under,' neither: for it came up as naturally to the surface as her Humour. My mother always said that one great charm in her was, her Naturalness.

If you read to your Company, pray do you ever read *the* Scene in the 'Spanish Tragedy' quoted in C. Lamb's Specimens—such a Scene as (not being in Verse, and quite familiar talk) I cannot help reading to my Guests—very few and far between—I mean by 'I,' one who has no gift at all for reading except the feeling of a few things: and I can't help stumbling upon Tears in this. Nobody knows who wrote this one scene: it was thought Ben Jonson, who could no more have written it than I who read it: for what else of his is it like? Whereas, Webster one fancies might have done it. It is not likely that you do not know this wonderful bit: but, if you have it not by heart almost, look for it again at once, and make others do so by reading to them. . . .

. . .Now, if I could send you part of what I am now packing up for some Woodbridge People—some— some—Saffron Buns!—for which this Place is notable from the first day of Lent till Easter—A little Hamper of these !

Now, my dear Mrs. Kemble, do consider this letter of mine as an Answer to yours—your two—else I shall be really frightened at making you write so often to yours always and sincerely

E. F.G.

LOWESTOFT : *April* 9/75.

DEAR MRS. KEMBLE,

...It has been indeed the Devil of a Winter : and even now—To-day as I write—no better than it was three months ago. The Daffodils scarce dare take April, let alone March ; and I wait here till a Green Leaf shows itself about Woodbridge.

I have been looking over four of Shakespeare's Plays, edited by Clark and Wright : editors of the 'Cambridge Shakespeare.' These 'Select Plays' are very well done, I think : Text, and Notes ; although with somewhat too much of the latter. Hamlet, Macbeth, Tempest, and Shylock—I heard them talking in my room—all alive about me.

By the by—How did *you* read 'To-morrow and To-morrow, etc.' All the Macbeths I have heard took the opportunity to become melancholy when they came to this : and, no doubt, some such change from Fury and Desperation was a relief to the Actor, and perhaps to the Spectator. But I think it *should* all go in the same Whirlwind of Passion as the rest : Folly !—Stage Play !—Farthing Candle ; Idiot, etc. Macready used to drop his Truncheon when he heard of the Queen's Death, and stand with his Mouth open for some while—which didn't become him.

LOWESTOFT : *May* 16/75.

DEAR MRS. KEMBLE,

...Spedding says that Irving's Hamlet is simply—
hideous—a strong expression for Spedding to use.
But—(lest I should think his condemnation was only
the Old Man's fault of depreciating all that is new),
he extols Miss Ellen Terry's Portia as simply *a perfect
Performance :* remembering (he says) all the while
how fine was Fanny Kemble's. Now, all this you
shall read for yourself, when I have token of your
Whereabout, and Howabout : for I will send you
Spedding's Letter, as well as his Paper.

Spedding won't go and see Salvini's Othello, because
he does not know Italian, and also because he hears
that Salvini's is a different Conception of Othello from
Shakespeare's. I can't understand either reason ; but
Spedding is (as Carlyle wrote me of his Bacon) the
'invincible, and victorious.' At any rate, I can't
beat him. Irving I never could believe in as Hamlet,
after seeing part of his famous Performance of a
Melodrama called ' The Bells ' three or four years ago.
But the Pollocks, and a large World beside, think
him a Prodigy—whom Spedding thinks—a Monster !
To this Complexion is the English Drama come.

I wonder if your American Winter has transformed
itself to such a sudden Summer as here in Old
England. I returned to my Woodbridge three weeks
ago : not a leaf on the Trees : in ten days they were
all green, and people—perspiring, I suppose one
must say. Now again, while the Sun is quite as Hot,
the Wind has swerved round to the East—so as one

broils on one side and freezes on t'other—and I—
the Great Twalmley —am keeping indoors from an
Intimation of Bronchitis.   I think it is time for one
to leave the Stage oneself. . . .

To W. F. Pollock.

LOWESTOFT, *Sept.* 22, [1875].

MY DEAR POLLOCK,

I brought here some Volumes of Lever's 'Cor-
nelius O'Dowd' Essays, very much better reading
than Addison, I think.   Also some of Sainte
Beuve's better than either.   A sentence in O'Dowd
reminded me of your Distrust of Civil Service
Examinations : 'You could not find a worse
Pointer than the Poodle which would pick you
out all the letters of the Alphabet.'   And is not
this pretty good of the World we live in ?   'You
ask me if I am going to " *The Masquerade.*"   I am
at it : Circumspice !'

So I pick out and point to other Men's Game,
this Sunday Morning, when the Sun makes the
Sea shine, and a strong head wind drives the Ships
with shortened Sail across it.   Last night I was
with some Sailors at the Inn : some one came
in who said there was a Schooner with five feet
water in her in the Roads : and off they went
to see if anything beside water could be got out
of her.   But, as you·say, one mustn't be epigram-
matic and clever.   Just before Grog and Pipe,

the Band had played some German Waltzes, a bit of Verdi, Rossini's ' Cujus animam,' and a capital Sailors' Tramp - chorus from Wagner, all delightful to me, on the Pier : how much better than all the dreary oratorios going on all the week at Norwich; Elijah, St. Peter, St. Paul, Eli, etc. There will be an Oratorio for every Saint and Prophet; which reminds me of my last Story. Voltaire had an especial grudge against Habakkuk. Some one proved to him that he had misrepresented facts in Habakkuk's history. ' C'est égal,' says V., ' Habakkuk était capable de tout.' Cornewall Lewis, who (like most other Whigs) had no Humour, yet tells this : I wonder if it will reach Dresden.

To E. B. Cowell.

[1875.]

MY DEAR COWELL,

. . . I told Elizabeth, I think, all I had to write about Arthur C. I had a letter from him a few days ago, hoping to see me in London, where I thought I might be going about this time, and where I would not go without giving him notice to meet me, poor lad. As yet however I cannot screw my Courage to go up : I have no Curiosity about what is to be seen or heard there ; my Day is done. I have not been very well all this Summer, and fancy that I begin to ' smell the Ground,' as Sailors say of the Ship that slackens speed as the Water shallows under her. I can't say I have much care for long Life : but still less for long Death : I mean a lingering one.

Did you ever read Madame de Sévigné ? I never did till this summer, rather repelled by her perpetual harping on her Daughter. But it is all genuine, and the same intense Feeling expressed in a hundred natural yet graceful ways : and beside all this such good Sense, good Feeling, Humour, Love of Books and Country Life, as makes her certainly the Queen of all Letter writers

WOODBRIDGE: *Febr : 2/76.*

Now, my dear Mrs. Kemble, I have done you a little good turn. Some days ago I was talking to my Brother John (I dared not show him !) of what you had said of my Family in your Gossip. He was extremely interested : and wished much that I [would] convey you his old hereditary remembrances. But, beside that, he wished you to have a Miniature of your Mother which my Mother had till she died. It is a full length ; in a white Dress, with blue Scarf, looking and tending with extended Arms upward in a Blaze of Light. My Brother had heard my Mother's History of the Picture, but could not recall it. I fancy it was before your Mother's Marriage. The Figure is very beautiful, and the Face also : like your Sister Adelaide, and your Brother Henry both. I think you will be pleased with this : and my Brother is very pleased that you should have it. Now, how to get it over to you is the Question; I believe I must get my little Quaritch, the Bookseller, who has a great American connection, to get it safely over to you. But if you know of any surer means, let me know. It is framed: and would look much better if some black edging were streaked into the Gold Frame; a thing I sometimes do only with a strip of Black Paper. The old Plan of Black and Gold Frames is much wanted where Yellow predominates in the Picture. Do you know I have a sort of Genius for Picture-framing, which is an Art People may despise, as they do the Milliner's: but you know how the prettiest Face may be hurt, and the plainest improved, by the Bonnet; and I find that (like the Bonnet, I suppose) you can only judge of the Frame, by trying it on. I used to tell some Picture Dealers they had better hire me for such Millinery: but I have not had much Scope for my Art down here. So now you have a little Lecture along with the Picture.

To C. E. Norton.

[WOODBRIDGE. *Feb.* 7/76.]

MY DEAR SIR,

. . . .Dante's face I have not seen these ten years: only his Back on my Book Shelf. What Mr. Lowell says of him recalled to me what Tennyson said to me some thirty-five or forty years ago. We were stopping before a shop in Regent Street where were two Figures of Dante and Goethe. I (I suppose) said, 'What is there in old Dante's Face that is missing in Goethe's?' And Tennyson (whose Profile then had certainly a remarkable likeness to Dante's) said : 'The Divine.' Then Milton; I don't think I've read him these forty years; the whole Scheme of the Poem, and certain Parts of it, looming as grand as anything in my Memory ; but I never could read ten lines together without stumbling at some Pedantry that tipped me at once out of Paradise, or even Hell, into the Schoolroom, worse than either. Tennyson again used to say that the two grandest of all Similes were those of the Ships hanging in the Air, and 'the Gunpowder one,' which he used slowly and grimly to enact, in the Days that are no more. He certainly then thought Milton the sublimest of all the Gang ; his Diction modelled on Virgil, as perhaps Dante's.

Spenser I never could get on with, and (spite of Mr. Lowell's good word) shall still content myself with such delightful Quotations from him as one lights upon here and there : the last from Mr. Lowell.

Then, old ' Daddy Wordsworth,' as he was some- times called, I am afraid, from my Christening, he is now, I suppose, passing under the Eclipse consequent on the Glory which followed his obscure Rise. I remember fifty years ago at our Cambridge, when the Battle was fighting for him by the Few against the Many of us who only laughed at ' Louisa in the

Shade,' etc. His Brother was then Master of Trinity College; like all Wordsworths (unless the drowned Sailor) pompous and priggish. He used to drawl out the Chapel responses so that we called him the 'Mēēserable Sinner' and his brother the 'Meeserable Poet.' Poor fun enough: but I never can forgive the Lakers all who first despised, and then patronized 'Walter Scott,' as they loftily called him: and. He, dear, noble, Fellow, thought they were quite justified. Well, your Emerson has done him far more Justice than his own Countryman Carlyle, who won't allow him to be a Hero in any way, but sets up such a can tankerous narrow-minded Bigot as John Knox in his stead. I did go to worship at Abbotsford, as to Stratford on Avon: and saw that it was good to have so done. If you, if Mr. Lowell, have not lately read it, pray read Lockhart's account of his Journey to Douglas Dale on (I think) July 18 or 19, 1831. It is a piece of Tragedy, even to the muttering Thunder, like the Lammermuir, which does not look very small beside Peter Bell and Co.

My dear Sir, this is a desperate Letter; and that last Sentence will lead to another dirty little Story about my Daddy: to which you must listen or I should feel like the Fine Lady in one of Vanbrugh's Plays, 'Oh my God, that you won't listen to a Woman of Quality when her Heart is bursting with Malice!' And perhaps you on the other Side of the Great Water may be amused with a little of your old Granny's Gossip.

Well then : about 1826, or 7, Professor Airy (now our Astronomer Royal) and his Brother William called on the Daddy at Rydal. In the course of Conversation Daddy mentioned that sometimes when genteel Parties came to visit him, he contrived to slip out of the room, and down the garden walk to where 'The Party's' travelling Carriage stood. This Carriage he would look into to see what Books they carried with them : and he observed it was generally 'WALTER SCOTT's.' It was Airy's Brother (a very veracious man, and an Admirer of Wordsworth, but, to be sure, more of Sir Walter) who told me this. It is this conceit that diminishes Wordsworth's stature among us, in spite of the mountain Mists he lived among. Also, a little stinginess ; not like Sir Walter in that ! I remember Hartley Coleridge telling us at Ambleside how Professor Wilson and some one else (H. C. himself perhaps) stole a Leg of Mutton from Wordsworth's Larder for the fun of the Thing.

To Mrs. Cowell.

12 MARINE TERRACE, LOWESTOFT.
April 8/76.

. . . If you go to Brittany you must go to my dear Sévigné's 'Rochers.' If I had the 'Go' in me, I should get there this Summer too : as to Abbotsford and Stratford. She has been my Companion here ; quite alive in the Room with me. I sometimes lament I did not know her before : but perhaps such an Acquaintance comes in best to cheer one toward the End.

[LOWESTOFT, April, 1876.]

MY DEAR MRS. KEMBLE,

From Lowestoft still I date : as just ten years ago when I was about building a Lugger, and reading Montaigne. The latter holds his own with me after three hundred years : and the Lugger does not seem much the worse for her ten years' wear, so well did she come bouncing between the Piers here yesterday, under a strong Sou'-Wester. My Great Captain has her no more; he has what they call a 'Scotch Keel' which is come into fashion : her too I see : and him too steering her, broader and taller than all the rest : fit to be a Leader of Men, Body and Soul; looking now Ulysses-like. Two or three years ago he had a run of constant bad luck ; and, being always of a grand convivial turn, treating Everybody, he got deep in Drink, against all his Promises to me, and altogether so lawless, that I brought things to a pass between us. ' He should go on with me if he would take the Tee-total Pledge for one year '—' No—he had broken his word,' he said, 'and he would not pledge it again,' much as he wished to go on with me. That, you see, was very fine in him ; he is altogether fine—A Great Man, I maintain it : like one of Carlyle's old Norway Kings, with a wider morality than we use ; which is very good and fine (as this Captain said to me) 'for you who are born with a silver spoon in your mouths.' `I did not forget what Carlyle too says about Great Faults in Great Men: even in David, the Lord's Anointed. But I thought best to share the Property with him and let him go his way. He had always resented being under any Control, and was very glad to be his own sole Master again: and yet clung to me in a wild and pathetic way. He has not been doing better since: and I fear is sinking into disorder.

This is a long story about one you know nothing about except what little I have told you. But the Man is a very remarkable Man indeed, and you may be interested—you must be—in him.

'Ho! parlons d'autres choses, ma 'Fille,' as my dear Sévigné says. She now occupies Montaigne's place in my room: well—worthily: she herself a Lover of Montaigne, and with a spice of his free thought and speech in her. I am sometimes vext I never made her acquaintance till last year: but perhaps it was as well to have such an acquaintance reserved for one's latter years. The fine Creature! much more alive to me than most Friends—I *should* like to see her 'Rochers' in Brittany.

To C. E. Norton.

LITTLE GRANGE, WOODBRIDGE.
June 10 [1], [1876].

MY DEAR SIR,

. . .Only a week ago I began my dear Don Quixote over again; as welcome and fresh as the Flowers of May. The Second Part is my favorite, in spite of what Lamb and Coleridge (I think) say; when, as old Hallam says, Cervantes has fallen in Love with the Hero whom he began by ridiculing. When this Letter is done I shall get out into my Garden with him, Sunday though it be.

We have also Memoirs of Godwin, very dry, I think; indeed with very little worth reading, except two or three Letters of dear Charles Lamb, 'Saint Charles,' as Thackeray once called him, while looking at one of his half-mad Letters, and remember[ing] his Devotion to that quite mad Sister. I must say I think his Letters infinitely better than his Essays; and Patmore says his Conversation, when just enough animated by Gin and Water, was better than either: which I believe too. Procter said he was far beyond the Coleridges, Wordsworths, Southeys, etc. And I am afraid I believe that also.

I am afraid too this is a long letter nearly [all] about my own Likes and Dislikes. 'The Great Twalmley's.'[1] But I began only thinking about Wordsworth. Pray do believe that I do not wish you to write unless you care to answer on that score. And now for the Garden and the Don: always in a common old Spanish Edition. Their coarse prints always make him look more of the Gentleman than the better Artists of other Countries have hitherto done.

Carlyle, I hear, is pretty well, though somewhat shrunk: scolding away at Darwin, The Turk, etc.

WOODBRIDGE: *Sept*. 21/76.

DEAR MRS. KEMBLE,

Have your American Woods begun to hang
out their Purple and Gold yet? on this Day of
Equinox. Some of ours begin to look rusty, after
the Summer Drought; but have not turned Yellow
yet. I was talking of this to a Heroine of mine who
lives near here, but visits the Highlands of Scotland,
which she loves better than Suffolk—and she said of
those Highland Trees—' O, they give themselves no
dying Airs, but turn Orange in a Day, and are swept
off in a Whirlwind, and Winter is come.'

Now too one's Garden begins to be haunted by
that Spirit which Tennyson says is heard talking to
himself among the flower-borders. Do you remember
him? [1]

And now—Who should send in his card to me
last week—but the old Poet himself—he and his
elder Son Hallam passing through Woodbridge from
a Tour in Norfolk. [2] ' Dear old Fitz,' ran the Card
in pencil, 'We are passing thro'.' [3] I had not seen
him for twenty years—he looked much the same,
except for his fallen Locks; and what really surprised
me was, that we fell at once into the old Humour,
as if we had only been parted twenty Days instead of
so many Years. I suppose this is a Sign of Age—
not altogether desirable. But so it was. He stayed
two Days, and we went over the same old grounds
of Debate, told some of the old Stories, and all was
well. I suppose I may never see him again: and
so I suppose we both thought as the Rail carried

him off: and each returned to his ways as if scarcely diverted from them. Age again!—I liked Hallam much; unaffected, unpretending—no Slang—none of Young England's nonchalance — speaking of his Father as 'Papa' and tending him with great Care, Love, and Discretion. Mrs. A. T. is much out of health, and scarce leaves Home, I think. . . .

LOWESTOFT: *October* 24/76.

DEAR MRS. KEMBLE,

Little—Nothing—as I have to write, I am nevertheless beginning to write to you, from this old Lodging of mine, from which I think our Correspondence chiefly began—ten years ago. I am in the same Room: the same dull Sea moaning before me: the same Wind screaming through the Windows: so I take up the same old Story. My Lugger was then about building:[1] she has passed into other hands now: I see her from time to time bouncing into Harbour, with her '244' on her Bows. Her Captain and I have parted: I thought he did very wrongly—Drink, among other things: but he did not think he did wrong: a different Morality from ours—that, indeed, of Carlyle's ancient Sea Kings. I saw him a few days ago in his house, with Wife and Children; looking, as always, too big for his house: but always grand, polite, and unlike anybody else. I was noticing the many Flies in the room—'Poor things,' he said, 'it is the warmth of our Stove makes them alive.' When Tennyson was with me, whose Portrait hangs

in my house in company with those of Thackeray
and this Man (the three greatest men I have known),
I thought that both Tennyson and Thackeray were
inferior to him in respect of Thinking of Themselves.
When Tennyson was telling me of how The Quarterly
abused him (humorously too), and desirous of knowing why one did not care for his later works, etc.,
I thought that if he had lived an active Life, as Scott
and Shakespeare; or even ridden, shot, drunk, and
played the Devil, as Byron, he would have done
much more, and talked about it much less. 'You
know,' said Scott to Lockhart, 'that I don't care a
Curse about what I write,'[1] and one sees he did not.
I don't believe it was far otherwise with Shakespeare.
Even old Wordsworth, wrapt up in his Mountain
mists, and proud as he was, was above all this vain
Disquietude: proud, not vain, was he: and that a
Great Man (as Dante) has some right to be—but not
to care what the Coteries say. What a Rigmarole!..

LITTLE GRANGE : WOODBRIDGE.

May 5/77.

DEAR MRS. KEMBLE,

Now, if when London is hot you should like to run
down to this Woodbridge, here will be my house at
your Service after July. It may be so all this month:
but a Nephew, Wife, and Babe did talk of a Fortnight's Visit: but have not talked of it since I
returned a fortnight ago. June and July my Invalid
Niece and her Sister occupy the House—not longer.

213

Donne, and all who know me, know that I do not like anyone to come out of their way to visit me : but, if they be coming this way, I am very glad to do my best for them. And if any of them likes to occupy my house at any time, here it is at their Service—at yours, for as long as you will, except the times I have mentioned. I give up the house entirely except my one room, which serves for Parlour and Bed : and which I really prefer, as it reminds me of the Cabin of my dear little Ship—mine no more. . . .

To C. E. Norton.

WOODBRIDGE. *August* 21/77.

MY DEAR SIR,

You have doubtless heard from Mr. Lowell since he got to Spain : he may have mentioned that un-accomplished visit to me which he was to have under-taken at your Desire. I doubt the two letters I wrote to be given him in London (through Quaritch) did not reach him : only the first which said my house was full of Nieces, so as I must lodge him (as I did our Laureate) at the Inn : but the second Letter was to say that I had Houseroom, and would meet him at the Train any day and hour. He wrote to me the day before he left for Paris to say that he had never intended to do more than just run down for the Day, shake hands, and away ! That I had an Instinct against : that one half-day's meeting of two Septua-genarians (I believe), to see one another's face for that once, 'But here, upon that Bank and Shoal of Time and ' then, ' jump the Life to come ' as well as the Life before.   No : I say I am glad he did not do that : but I had my house all ready to entertain him as best I could ; and had even planned a little Visit to our neighbouring Coast, where are the Village remains of a once large Town devoured by the Sea : and, yet undevoured (except by Henry VIII.), the grey walls of a Grey Friars' Priory, beside which they used to walk, under such Sunsets as illumine them still.   This pathetic Ruin, still remaining by the Sea, would (I feel sure) have been more to one from the New Atlantis than all London can show : but I should have liked better had Mr. Lowell seen it on returning to America, rather than going to Spain, where the yet older and more splendid Moors would soon have effaced the memory of our poor Dunwich. If you have a Map of England, look for it on the Eastern Coast.   If Mr. Lowell should return this way, and return in the proper Season for such cold Climate as ours, he shall see it : and so shall you, if you will, under like conditions ; including a reasonable and available degree of Health in myself to do the honours. . . .

I live down in such a Corner of this little Country that I see scarce any one but my Woodbridge Fellow-townsmen, and learn but little from such Friends as could tell me of the World beyond.   But the English do not generally love Letter writing : and very few of us like it the more as we get older.   So I have but

little to say that deserves an Answer from you : but
please to write me a little : a word about Mr. Lowell,
whom you have doubtless heard from.   [One politeness I had prepared for him here was, to show him
some sentences in his Books which I did not like !]
Which also leads me to say that some one sent me a
number of your American ' Nation ' with a Review of
my redoubtable Agamemnon : written by a superior
hand, and, I think, quite discriminating in its dis-
tribution of Blame and Praise : though I will not say
the Praise was not more than deserved ; but it was
where deserved, I think.

WOODBRIDGE, *October* 10/77.

MY DEAR WRIGHT,

I bid Adieu to Dunwich last Monday : the Sea
running up to the Cliffs before a North wind and a
Spring tide. The place was still delightful, with but
a Friend to look in upon of an evening : but Edwards
and Wife left the day I did.   They are staying at
Framlingham for a few days, his Nation (which, by
the way, is good Boccaccio Italian as well as good
Suffolk), and where he fancied he would make a
sketch of the Castle. She would let me know, if she
could, when they left : but he is become impatient in
his ways : and they may be in London by this time,
for aught I know.

One day ask some of your mathematic Friends to
tell you, and then me, how the Moon was on the

night of Sept. 3/1650, night before the Battle of Dunbar. She does so much in Carlyle's fine account, 'wading through the Clouds,' etc., that I want to know how old she was at the time. He does not, I think, quote from any contemporary as to this : and as I see in his French Revolution that he represents the Pleiads and Orion looking down on the streets of Paris on the Night of August 9, he may have supplied to Dunbar a more considerable moon than the Almanack authorises. But it is a very fine book.

To C. E. Norton.

WOODBRIDGE. *April 4, 1878.*

MY DEAR NORTON,

I wish you would not impose on yourself to write me a Letter ; which you say is 'in your head.' You have Literary work, and a Family to enjoy with you what spare time your Professional Studies leave you. Whereas I have nothing of any sort that I am engaged to do : all alone for months together : taking up such Books as I please ; and rather liking to write Letters to my Friends, whom I now only communicate with by such means. And very few of my oldest Friends, here in England, care to answer me, though I know from no want of Regard : but I know that few sensible men, who have their own occupations, care to write Letters unless on some special purpose ; and I now rarely get more than one yearly Letter from each. Seeing which, indeed, I now rarely trouble them for more. So pray be at ease in this respect : you have written to me, as I to you, more than has passed between myself and my fifty years old Friends for some years past...

Now I enclose you a little work of mine [1] which I hope does no irreverence to the Man it talks of. It is meant quite otherwise. I often got puzzled, in reading Lamb's Letters, about some Data in his Life to which the Letters referred : so I drew up the enclosed for my own behoof, and then thought that others might be glad of it also. If I set down his Miseries, and the one Failing for which those Miseries are such a Justification, I only set down what has been long and publickly known, and what, except in a Noodle's eyes, must enhance the dear Fellow's character, instead of lessening it. ' Saint Charles ! ' said Thackeray to me thirty years ago, putting one of C. L.'s letters [1] to his forehead ; and old Wordsworth said of him : ' If there be a Good Man, Charles Lamb is one.'. . .

---

[1] Charles Lamb. A calendar of his life in four pages.

EDWARD FITZGERALD

April 16, [1878].

[Where, by the by, I heard the Nightingale for the first time yesterday Morning. That is, I believe, almost its exact date of return, wind and weather permitting. Which being premised—]

Dear Mrs. Kemble,

I think it is about the time for you to have a letter from me; for I think I am nearly as punctual as the Nightingale, though at quicker Intervals; and perhaps there may be other points of Unlikeness. After hearing that first Nightingale in my Garden, I found a long, kind, and pleasant, Letter from Mr. Lowell in Madrid: the first of him too that I have heard since he flew thither. Just before he wrote, he says, he had been assigning Damages to some American who complained of having been fed too long on Turtle's Eggs :—and all that sort of Business, says the Minister, does not inspire a man to Letter-writing. He is acclimatizing himself to Cervantes, about whom he must write one of his fine, and (as I think) final Essays: I mean such as (in the case of others he has done) ought to leave no room for a reversal of Judgment. Amid the multitude of Essays, Reviews, etc., one still wants *that*: and I think Lowell does it more than any other Englishman. He says he meets Valasquez at every turn of the street; and Murillo's Santa Anna opens his door for him. Things are different here : but when my Oracle last night was reading to me of Dandie Dinmont's

blessed visit to Bertram in Portanferry Gaol, I said—
'I know it's Dandie, and I shouldn't be at all surprized
to see him come into this room.' No—no more than
—Madame de Sévigné! I suppose it is scarce right
to live so among Shadows; but—after near seventy
years so passed—' Que voulez-vous?'

Still, if any Reality would—of its own Volition—
draw near to my still quite substantial Self; I say
that my House (if the Spring do not prove unkindly)
will be ready to receive—and the owner also—any
time before June, and after July; that is, before Mrs.
Kemble goes to the Mountains, and after she returns
from them. I dare say no more, after so much so
often said, and all about oneself.

Yesterday the Nightingale; and To-day a small,
still, Rain which we had hoped for, to make 'poindre'
the Flower-seeds we put in Earth last Saturday. All
Sunday my white Pigeons were employed in confis-
cating the Sweet Peas we had laid there; so that
To-day we have to sow the same anew.

To F. Tennyson.

WOODBRIDGE, *May* 8/78.

MY DEAR FREDERIC,

...I suppose you see the Athenæum or some such
Paper as tells you of new Books, etc. The last
Athenæum gave a remarkable account of Trelawny's
reprint of his remarkable account of Shelley and

Byron, published over thirty years ago, I think. He seems to have loved Shelley as a Man : Byron, not so well : which I think one can sympathise with. The Cockneys are now making a tremendous effort to set up Shelley as *the* Apollo of his time : for a true Poet I recognise him : but too unsubstantial for me : and poor Keats' little finger worth all his Body : not to mention Byron, with all his faults. Lord Houghton (Dicky Milnes of old) sent me some years ago Keats' first Draught of the opening of Hyperion, printed from a MS. which he (Lord H.) had, but which was stolen from him by one of his many Friends. This I would post you if you cared to see it. But I really don't know if my doing so be not a bore to you.

I fancy we must now be having Jersey weather here : very warm and wet. All our younger trees are in leaf, fresh if not full : the old Oaks and Elms, whose blood, I suppose, circulates more slowly, still reserving themselves. I have been kept in for two days ; and, as my Eyes happen to be rusty just now, am rather puzzled how to get through the Day—

> And hence arises ancient Men's Report—
> The Days are tedious, but the Years are short.

So says old Crabbe : who elsewhere says :

> So with the aid that Shops and Sailing [Books and
>   Letters ?] give,
> Life passes on—'tis Labour—but we live.

There is Mark Tapley for you, at his favourite re-creation.

I saw another Copy of your Days and Hours in a Bristol Catalogue; sent for it, but it had been sold. You know I have the large Volume from which the publisht one was drawn: but I buy the latter to give away. I see your old friend Browning is in the field again, with another of his odd titles: De Saisiez—or Croisic—or some such name. I tried to read his Dramatic Lyrics again: they seemed to me Ingoldsby Legends.

To W. A. Wright.

WOODBRIDGE. *June* 11, [1878].

MY DEAR WRIGHT,

If you do not remember the passage in Bacon's Essays[1] about 'not to decide, etc.' I must have fancied it. I am glad you recognize the Othello bit of Montaigne. You know, as I know, the non-sense of talking of Shakespeare stealing such things: one is simply pleased at finding his footsteps in the Books he read, just as one is in walking over the fields he walked about Stratford and seeing the Flowers, and hearing the Birds, he heard and saw, and told of. My Canon is, there is no plagiarism when he who adopts has proved that he could originate what he adopts, and a great deal more: which certainly absolves Shakespeare from any such Charge—even 'The Cloud capt Towers, etc.' That

[1] Not in the Essays but in the Colours of Good and Evil, 4: 'For as he sayth well, *Not to resolve is to resolve.*'

Passage in Othello about the Propontic and the Hellespont, was, I have read, an afterthought, after reading some Travel : and, like so many Afterthoughts, I must think, a Blunder : breaking the Torrent of Passion with a piece of Natural History. One observes it particularly when acted : the actor down on his Knees, etc. Were I to act Othello (there'd be many a Bellow

From Pit, Boxes, etc., on that occasion) I should leave out the passage. . . .

To E. B. Cowell.

[*July* 3, 1878.]

MY DEAR COWELL,

Our Letters crossed, you see. It is rather a Shame for me to be writing to you the day after my last : I think I shall become rather a Bore, for I certainly do write Letters which I should not if I had proper occupation, and I can't much edify those I write to. Only yesterday I sent Wright some lines from Ronsard, quoted in Southey's C.P. Book, showing that R. had read Lucretius, who, with his Editor, has been in my mind for the last month and more. My Reader comes at 8 P.M. and reads me Arctic Voyages and such like ; is now reading me a pleasant Book—Round my House—by one Hamerton, who goes to live in middle France—Autun, I make out his City to be—describing his French Neighbours pleasantly, so far as we have gone. We have also

223

read the Heart of Midlothian. How can people set up their Austens, Eliots, Brontës, etc., not only with, but above, these early Scotch Novels! . . . I know there is plenty of tiresome in these Books, bores like Saddletree, as in Life itself, some theatrical falsity too; but, altogether!—I was glad to have seen Edinburgh and Arthur's Seat.

Which leads me to your Welsh Holyday; which set me upon writing this upon receipt of your Letter. For it makes me a little sad that now I never meet you in these Summer times: which is my fault, not yours. But, were I in Wales, I should not manage foot rambles even as well as heretofore, and so stay in old flat Suffolk. You do well, I think, in sticking to one Change, once finding that it suits you; not hunting about for others. 'Leave Well alone.' I hope that you will soon be off, though the weather is cool now.

I have not had heart to go on our river since the death of my old Companion West, with whom I had traversed reach after reach for these dozen Years. I am almost as averse to them now as Peter Grimes. So now I content myself with the River side. All which, I begin to think, I must have written to you yesterday: so here is a bit of the Bore one finds in Scott, and real Life.

This has been a bad Year with Gardens hereabout: Roses especially snubbed by some Frosts in June. This evening the Children of St. John's Parish are coming to play in *My Grounds!* and I do wish the

Cloud would pack away for the occasion. I have a large Barn cleared out, and a Swing fixt on a Beam: that is all my Share in the Expenses. But then—*My Grounds!*

To W. A. Wright.

13 DENMARK ROAD, LOWESTOFT,
Sept. 21 [1878].

MY DEAR WRIGHT,

...I have taken two rooms at Dix Hall for July, August, September, so as I may run to and fro at will. Edwards seems pretty well, and has Pictures of Walberswick at the Academy; Sky high. 'By Gode!' as Fuseli said, 'they have sent him to Heaven before his time.' This Paper, suitable to the Season, comes handy to my Eyes, which are not by any means the freshest. . . .

To C. E. Norton.

WOODBRIDGE. *October* 15/78.

MY DEAR NORTON,

. . . I got little more than a Fortnight at that old Dunwich; for my Landlady took seriously ill, and finally died: and the Friend [1] whom I went to meet there became so seriously ill also as to be obliged to return to London before August was over. So then I went to an ugly place [2] on the sea shore also, some fifteen miles off the old Priory; and there was with

[1] Edwin Edwards.   [2] Lowestoft.

some Nephews and Nieces, trying to read the Novels from a Circulating Library with indifferent Success. And now here am I at home once more ; getting my Garden, if not my House, in order ; and here I shall be probably all Winter, except for a few days visit to that sick Friend in London, if he desires it. . . .

We too have been having a Fortnight of delightful weather, so as one has been able to sit abroad all the Day. And now, that Spirit which Tennyson sung of in one of his early Poems is heard, as it were, walking and talking to himself among the decaying flower - beds. This Season (such as we have been enjoying)—my old Crabbe sings of it too, in a very pathetic way to me : for it always seems to me an Image of the Decline of Life also.

> It was a Day ere yet the Autumn closed,
> When Earth before her Winter's War reposed ;
> When from the Garden as we look'd above,
> No Cloud was seen, and nothing seem'd to move ;
> [When the wide River was a silver Sheet,
> And upon Ocean slept the unanchored fleet ;]
> When the wing'd Insect settled in our sight,
> And waited wind to recommence its flight.

You see I cross out two lines which, fine as they are, go beyond the Garden : but I am not sure if I place them aright. The two last lines you will feel, I think : for I suppose some such Insect is in America too. (You must not mind Crabbe's self-contradiction about ' nothing moving.') . . .

To Charles Merivale.

WOODBRIDGE, *December* 15 [1878].

MY DEAR DEAN,

Donne gave me your letter when I last saw him, on Friday afternoon. My scrap appended to his letter did not deserve so good acknowledgment from you: so now, you see, I try to make up for it, especially as you in some measure ask me about Mrs. Kemble.

I did not see much of her acting, nor hear much of her reading, for in truth I did not much admire either. She herself admits she had no liking for the stage, and (in a capital paper in some magazine) that she had not a *Theatrical* gift, though she had, she thinks, a *Dramatic*, a distinction which I leave for herself to explain. In such readings of hers as I heard, she seemed to me to do the men and the soldiers best, such as the warlike lords in King John. I did not hear her Hotspur, which should have been good, as was her brother Jack's at school. I never heard such capital declamation as *his* Hotspur, and Alexander's Feast, when we were at Bury together, he about eighteen, and then with the profile of Alexander himself, as I have seen it on medals, etc. When *you* knew him he had lost, I suppose, his youthful freshness. His sister, Fanny, I say, I did not much admire in public: but she was, and is, a noble-hearted and noble-souled woman, however wayward; and no one more loyal, not only to her own, but to her brother's friends and schoolfellows. And does she not write finely too? Sometimes in long sentences too, which spin out without entanglement from her pen.

When I remember your viva voce, and when I read your letters, Merivale, I always wish some one would make notes of your table and letter talk : so witty, so humorous, so just. You would not do this yourself; if you thought about what you said and wrote for such a purpose it would not, I suppose, be as good ; but I wish others would do it for you—and—I must not say 'for *me*' at my time of day, but for those who come after us both.

I had not seen Donne for three years, I think : he seemed to me feebler in body and mind, but the same dear old Donne still.

And I am still yours, as his,

OLD FITZ.

To J. R. Lowell.

December 22.

I left off when my Reader came to finish The Bride of Lammermoor ; as wonderful to me as ever. O, the Austens, Eliots, and even Thackerays, won't eclipse Sir Walter for long.

To come down rather a little from him, my Calderon, which you speak of—very many beside myself, with as much fair Dramatic Spirit, knowledge of good English and English Verse, would do quite as well as you think I do, if they would not hamper themselves with Forms of Verse, and Thought, irreconcilable with English Language and English Ways of Thinking. I am persuaded that, to keep Life in the Work (as Drama must) the Translator (however inferior to his Original) must re-cast that original into his own Likeness, more or less : the less like his original, so much the worse : but still, the live Dog better than the dead Lion ; in Drama, I say. As to Epic, is not Cary still the best Dante ? Cowper and Pope were both Men of Genius, out of my Sphere ; but whose Homer still holds its own ? The elaborately exact, or the 'teacup-time' Parody ? Is not Fairfax' Tasso good ? I never read Harington's Ariosto, English or Italian. Another shot have I made at Faust in Bayard Taylor's Version : but I do not even get on with him as with Hayward, hampered as he (Taylor) is with his allegiance to original metres, etc. His Notes I was interested in : but I shall die ungoethed, I doubt, so far as Poetry goes : I always believe he was Philosopher and Critic. . .

WOODBRIDGE : *April* 3/79.

MY DEAR MRS. KEMBLE :—

...I am getting my 'Tales of the Hall' printed, and shall one day ask you, and three or four beside, whether it had better be published. I think you, and those three or four others, will like it ; but they

may also judge that indifferent readers might not.
And that you will all of you have to tell me when
the thing is done. I shall not be in the least
disappointed if you tell me to keep it among 'ourselves,' so long as 'ourselves' are pleased; for I
know well that Publication would not carry it much
further abroad; and I am very well content to pay
my money for the little work which I have long
meditated doing. I shall have done 'my little owl.'
Do you know what that means?—No. Well then;
my Grandfather had several Parrots of different sorts
and Talents: one of them ('Billy,' I think) could
only huff up his feathers in what my Grandfather
called an owl fashion; so when Company were
praising the more gifted Parrots, he would say—
'You will hurt poor Billy's feelings—Come! Do
your little owl, my dear!'—You are to imagine a
handsome, hair-powdered, Gentleman doing this—
and his Daughter—my Mother—telling of it.

And so it is I do my little owl.

This little folly takes a long bit of my Letter
paper—and I do not know that you will see any
fun in it. Like my Book, it would not tell in Public.

Spedding reads my proofs—for, though I have
confidence in my Selection of the Verse (owl), I
have but little in my interpolated Prose, which I
make obscure in trying to make short. Spedding
occasionally marks a blunder; but (confound him!)
generally leaves me to correct it.

Come—here is more than enough of my little owl.
At night we read Sir Walter for an Hour (Montrose

just now) by way of 'Play'—then 'ten minutes'
refreshment allowed'—and the Curtain rises on
Dickens (Copperfield now) which sends me gaily to
bed—after one Pipe of solitary Meditation—in which
the—'little owl,' etc.

By the way, in talking of Plays—after sitting with
my poor friend and his brave little Wife till it was
time for him to turn bedward—I looked in at the
famous Lyceum Hamlet; and soon had looked, and
heard, enough. It was incomparably the worst I
had ever witnessed, from Covent Garden down to
a Country Barn. I should scarce say this to you
if I thought you had seen it; for you told me you
thought Irving might have been even a great Actor,
from what you saw of his Louis XI. I think. When
he got to 'Something too much of this,' I called out
from the Pit door where I stood, 'A good deal too
much,' and not long after returned to my solitary inn...

WOODBRIDGE: *April 25*, [1879.]

DEAR MRS. KEMBLE,

...I—We—have finished all Sir Walter's Scotch
Novels; and I thought I would try an English one:
Kenilworth—a wonderful Drama, which Theatre,
Opera, and Ballet (as I once saw it represented)
may well reproduce. The Scene at Greenwich, where
Elizabeth 'interviews' Sussex and Leicester, seemed
to me as fine as what is called (I am told, wrongly)
Shakespeare's Henry VIII. Of course, plenty of

melodrama in most other parts :—but the Plot wonderful.

Then—after Sir Walter—Dickens' Copperfield, which came to an end last night because I would not let my Reader read the last Chapter. What a touch when Peggotty—the man—at last finds the lost Girl, and—throws a handkerchief over her face when he takes her to his arms—never to leave her! I maintain it—a little Shakespeare—a Cockney Shakespeare, if you will : but as distinct, if not so great, a piece of pure Genius as was born in Stratford. Oh, I am quite sure of that, had I to choose but one of them, I would choose Dickens' hundred delightful Caricatures rather than Thackeray's half-dozen terrible Photographs. . . .

To W. A. Wright.

38 MINERVA TERRACE, LOWESTOFT,
September 4 [1879].

MY DEAR WRIGHT,

Here have I been for three weeks, and Cowell at 9 Esplanade for some days more, wondering that we hear nothing of your coming. I suppose that he will not stay beyond next week ; after which he purposes running to Lincoln to see the Cathedral and some of his wife's old haunts for two or three days, and then back to Cambridge. We think you must have been having some tough work with your Yorkshire Farmers on account of these bad times. But let us know something of yourself, by letter if not in person.

We read Don Quixote for two or three hours of a Forenoon, and of course Cowell lights it all up as it was never lighted to me before. I do not walk with him, as my feet have been out of order, and besides I like a long interval of fallow, even after *his* company. So we meet again at night for two or three hours' chat. He has not found his Roman Nettle yet; but some other not very common flowers he has found, and rejoices in them like the great big Boy he is. I never saw him better in mind or Body. For some time he was afraid of venturing on the Pier because of Hans Breitman, who was staying at the Royal: but Hans is gone, and the Professor occasionally mixes in the gay crowd.

Do not miss Severn's letters about Keats in Athenæum.

11 MARINE TERRACE, LOWESTOFT,
September 11/79.

MY DEAR WRIGHT,

Cowell and I have read through Don Quixote's second part, down to where Sancho makes the Night-patrol of his Island. There, our Books fell short, and so there we stopped. Whether we shall ever finish it together? I think he and Wife have been happy enough here: I know they have made me so: and their departure to-day drives me rather sorrowfully back into my old Quarters. There—sc. here—

I shall be till the end of the month, I suppose : and young Arthur Charlesworth will come to me for his Holyday.

Yesterday this mad Professor was seized with a wish to talk Welsh with George Borrow : and, as he would not venture otherwise, I gave him a Note of Introduction, and off he went, and had an hour with the old Boy, who was hard of hearing, and shut up in a stuffy room, but cordial enough ; and Cowell was glad to have seen the Man, and tell him that it was his Wild Wales which first inspired a thirst for the Language into the Professor. Of all this he will himself tell you. For to-morrow (Friday) he will be at Scroope Terrace, after stopping a Night and a Day at Norwich, to see the Cathedral and St. Peter's Mancroft. I might accompany him so far, but my feet are much indisposed for walking just now, and I have no turn for sight-seeing. . . .

WOODBRIDGE : *Sept.* 28, [1879.]

DEAR MRS. KEMBLE :—

I cannot be sure of your Address : but I venture a note—to say that—If you return to London on Wednesday, I shall certainly run up (the same day, if I can) to see you before you again depart on Saturday, as your letter proposes.

But I also write to beg you not to leave your Daughter for ever so short a while, simply because you had so arranged, and told me of your Arrangement.

If this Note of mine reach you somehow to-morrow, there will be plenty of time for you to let me know whether you go or not: and, even if there be not time before Wednesday, why, I shall take no harm in so far as I really have a very little to do, and moreover shall see a poor Lady who has just lost her husband, after nearly three years anxious and uncertain watching, and now finds herself (brave and strong little Woman) somewhat floored now the long conflict is over. These are the people I may have told you of whom I have for some years met here and there in Suffolk—chiefly by the Sea; and we somehow suited one another. He was a brave, generous, Boy (of sixty) with a fine Understanding, and great Knowledge and Relish of Books: but he had applied too late in Life to Painting which he could not master, though he made it his Profession. A remarkable mistake, I always thought, in so sensible a man.

Whether I find you next week, or afterward (for I promise to find you any time you appoint) I hope to find you alone—for twenty years' Solitude make me very shy: but always your sincere

E. F.G.

LITTLE GRANGE : WOODBRIDGE.   *October* 7, [1879.]

DEAR MRS. KEMBLE,

When I got home yesterday, and emptied my Pockets, I found the precious Enclosure which I had meant to show, and (if you pleased) to give you. A wretched Sketch (whether by me or another, I know not) of your Brother John in some Cambridge Room, about the year 1832–3, when he and I were staying there, long after Degree time—he, studying Anglo-Saxon, I suppose—reading something, you see, with a glass of Ale on the table—or old Piano-forte was it?—to which he would sing very well his German Songs. Among them,

Do you remember? I afterwards associated it with some stray verses applicable to one I loved.

'Heav'n would answer all your wishes,
    Were it much as Earth is here ;
Flowing Rivers full of Fishes,
    And good Hunting half the Year.'

Well :—here is the cause of this Letter, so soon after our conversing together, face to face, in Queen Anne's Mansions. A strange little After-piece to twenty years' Separation.

And now, here are the Sweet Peas, and Marigolds, sown in the Spring, still in a faded Blossom, and the Spirit that Tennyson told us of fifty years ago haunting the Flower-beds, and a Robin singing—nobody else.

And I am to lose my capital Reader, he tells me, in a Fortnight, no Book-binding surviving under the pressure of Bad Times in little Woodbridge. 'My dear Fitz, there is no Future for little Country towns,' said Pollock to me when he came here some years ago.

But my Banker here found the Bond which he had considered unnecessary, safe in his Strong Box :—and I am your sincere Ancient

E. F.G.

Burn the poor Caricature if offensive to you. The 'Alexander' profile was become somewhat tarnished then.

To F. Tennyson.

WOODBRIDGE, *Oct.* 19 [1879].

MY DEAR FREDERIC,

It is a long time since I have heard from you, and I am pretty sure that I wrote last. I do not mean to claim a debt : but, however, I want to hear of you from yourself. A good slice of the year has fallen away since last I wrote, I know. Since which I have been to my old resort, Lowestoft, for near two months : five weeks of which my friend Edward Cowell, whom you remember, was there with his Wife : and we read Don Quixote of a Morning, and chatted together of a Night. And so *that* went. After which, I went up to London to see two bereaved Ladies : one of whom has just lost her husband, the brave Boy, and bad Painter, whom I have spent several weeks along with by our Shores for some years past——*Edwards*, his name : and then Mrs. Kemble, who has recently lost her Sister Mrs. Sartoris, whom you once heard sing Weber's Mermaid Song at Florence. Well, I had not seen Mrs. Kemble for over twenty years ; and she wished once more, she said, to see an old Friend of herself and her Family. So I went, and was four days in London visiting these two Ladies alternately ; and am now down again in Winter Quarters, I suppose. But my excellent Reader has left me in the lurch, and his successor is a younger Brother, not sixteen years old, with a boyish treble which sounds odd enunciating Trollope's Novels to me. It is sad to me to think that I have exhausted Scott ; and all of Dickens, except two which I reckoned on for this winter with my old Reader, who relished them as much as I. Well, we must try the Boy's pipe. When I was in London, I went to morning Service in Westminster Abbey : and, as I sat in the Poet's Corner Transept, I looked down for the stone that covers the remains of Charles Dickens, but it may have been covered by the worshippers there. I had not been inside that Abbey for twenty years, I believe ; and it seemed very grand to me ; and the old Organ rolled and swam with the Boys' voices on the Top through the fretted vault, as you know. Except *that*, I heard no music, and saw no Sights, save in the Streets.

If you did not see (as I dare say you did not)

old Spedding's preliminary Notice of your Brother Charles's Sonnets, I will send it to you. It has—it *must* have—fine things in it : but it is not calculated, I think, to propitiate those who previously knew little, or nothing, of him whom Spedding would recommend.

WOODBRIDGE : Nov. 13/79.

MY DEAR LADY,

...'Clerke Sanders' has been familiar to me these fifty years almost; since Tennyson used to repeat it, and 'Helen of Kirkconnel,' at some Cambridge gathering. At that time he looked something like the Hyperion shorn of his Beams in Keats' Poem: with a Pipe in his mouth. Afterwards he got a touch, I used to say, of Haydon's Lazarus. Talking of Keats, do not forget to read Lord Houghton's Life and Letters of him: in which you will find what you may not have guessed from his Poetry (though almost unfathomably deep in that also) the strong, masculine, Sense and Humour, etc., of the man: more akin to Shakespeare, I am tempted to think, in a perfect circle of Poetic Faculties, than any Poet since.

Well: the Leaves which hung on more bravely than ever I remember are at last whirling away in a Cromwell Hurricane—(not quite that, neither)—and my old Man says he thinks Winter has set in at last. We cannot complain hitherto. Many summer flowers held out in my Garden till a week ago, when we dug up the Beds in order for next year. So now little but

239

the orange Marigold, which I love for its colour (Irish and Spanish) and Courage, in living all Winter through...

WOODBRIDGE: *Febr:* 3/80.

MY DEAR LADY,

I do not think it is a full month since I last taxed you for some account of yourself : but we have had hard weather, you know, ever since : your days have been very dark in London, I am told, and as we have all been wheezing under them, down here, I want to know how you stand it all. I only hope my MS. is not very bad ; for I am writing by Candle, before my Reader comes. He eat such a Quantity of Cheese and Cake between the Acts that he could scarce even see to read at all after; so I had to remind him that, though he was not quite sixteen, he had much exceeded the years of a Pig. Since which we get on better. I did not at all like to have my Dombey spoiled; especially Captain Cuttle, God bless him, and his Creator, now lying in Westminster Abbey. The intended Pathos is, as usual, missed : but just turn to little Dombey's Funeral, where the Acrobat in the Street suspends his performance till the Funeral has passed, and his Wife wonders if the little Acrobat in her Arms will so far outlive the little Boy in the Hearse as to wear a Ribbon through his hair, following his Father's Calling. It is in such Side-touches, you know, that Dickens is inspired to Create like a little God Almighty. I have read half

240

his lately published letters, which, I think, add little to Forster's Account, unless in the way of showing what a good Fellow Dickens was. Surely it does not seem that his Family were not fond of him, as you supposed?

I have been to Lowestoft for a week to see my capital Nephew, Edmund Kerrich, before he goes to join his Regiment in Ireland. I wish you could see him make his little (six years old) put him through his Drill. That is worthy of Dickens: and I am always yours sincerely—and I do hope not just now very illegibly—

To W. A. Wright.

WOODBRIDGE, *Feb.* 23 [1880].

MY DEAR WRIGHT,

I have been to London for two days: perhaps you were in Jerusalem[1] at the same time. I put up at the Golden Cross, Charing Cross, a very cheerful, clean, well-ordered, and even quiet Quarters. I visited Mrs. Kemble every day, or Night rather: and also my poor dear Donne, who is decidedly feebler than I saw him in October. The only Theatre I looked into was that of the Aquarium, on my way from Mrs. Kemble: 'As You Like It' being played by Housemaids and Cooks, it seemed to me; a wonder to me, who yet had been apprised of what Shakespeare had fallen to. So that when some Hunting-horns began, and some men to sing, 'What shall he have that killed the

241

Deer ? ' to the good old Tune, I was fairly overset b
the reaction from detestable, and waited for no more

To Lord Houghton.

WOODBRIDGE. *May 10th* 1880.[2]

DEAR LORD HOUGHTON,

I think I have sent you a yearly letter of some
sort or other for several years, so it has come upon
me once again. I have nothing to ask of you except
how you are. I should just like to know that, including ' yours ' in you. Just a very few words will
suffice, and I daresay you have no time for more. I
have so much time that it is evident I have nothing
to tell, except that I have just entered upon a military
career in so far as having become much interested in
the battle of Waterloo, which I just remember a year
after it was fought, when a solemn anniversary took
place in a neighbouring parish where I was born, and
the village carpenter came to my father to borrow a
pair of Wellington boots for the lower limbs of a
stuffed effigy of Buonaparte, which was hung on a
gibbet, and guns and pistols were discharged at him,
while we and the parson of the parish sat in a tent
where we had beef and plum pudding and loyal
toasts. To this hour I remember the smell of the
new-cut hay in the meadow as we went in our best
summer clothes to the ceremony. But now I am
trying to understand whether the Guards or the 52nd

Regiment deserved most credit for *écraséing* the Imperial Guard. Here is a fine subject to address you on in the year 1880! Let it go for nothing; but just tell me how you are, and believe me, with some feeling of old, if not very close intimacy,

Yours sincerely,
EDWARD FITZGERALD.

To Charles Keene.

WOODBRIDGE. *Sunday.*

MY DEAR KEENE,

Your Letter reached me yesterday when I was just finishing my Sévigné; I mean, reading it over. I have plenty of Notes for an Introductory Argument and List of Dramatis Personæ, and a clue to the course of her Letters, so as to set a new reader off on the right tack, with some previous acquaintance with the People and Places she lives among. But I shrink from trying to put such Notes into shape; all writing always distasteful to me, and now very difficult, at seventy odd. Some such Introduction would be very useful: people being in general puzzled with Persons, Dates, etc., if not revolted by the eternal, though quite sincere, fuss about her Daughter, which the Eye gradually learns to skim over, and get to the fun. I felt a pang when arriving at—

Ci git
Marie de Rabutin-Chantal
Marquise de Sévigné
Décédée le 18 Avril 1696

still to be found, I believe, on a Tablet in the Church of Grignan in Provence. I have been half minded to run over to Brittany just to see Les Rochers; but a French 'Murray' informed me that the present owner will not let it be seen by Strangers attracted by all those 'paperasses,' as he calls her Letters. Probably I should not have gone in any case when it came to proof. . . .

I did not forget Waterloo Day. Just as I and my Reader Boy were going into the Pantry for some *grub*, I thought of young Ensign Leeke, not 18, who carried the Colours of that famous 52nd which gave the 'coup de grace' to the Imperial Guard about 8 p.m. and then marched to Rossomme, seeing the Battle was won : and the Colour-serjeant found some bread in some French Soldier's knapsack, and brought a bit to his Ensign, 'You must want a bit, Sir, and I am sure you have deserved it.' That was a Compliment worth having !

I have, like you, always have, and from a Child had, a mysterious feeling about that ' Sizewell Gap.' There were reports of kegs of Hollands found under the Altar Cloth of Theberton Church near by : and we Children looked with awe on the 'Revenue Cutters' which passed Aldbro', especially remembering one that went down with all hands, ' The Ranger.'

They have half spoilt Aldbro'; but now that Dunwich is crossed out from my visiting Book by the loss of that fine fellow,[1] whom this time of year

[1] Edwin Edwards.

especially reminds me of, I must return to Aldbro'
now and then. Why can't you go there with me?
I say no more of your coming here, for you ought to
be assured that you would be welcome at any time;
but I never do ask any busy, or otherwise engaged
man to come. . . .

Here is a good Warwickshire word—'I *sheered*
my Eyes round the room.' So good, that it explains
itself.

To F. Tennyson.

THE OLD PLACE, *June* [1880].

MY DEAR FREDERIC,

I did not send you the last Musical Times, because
it seemed to me less interesting than others which I
had sent you before. But yesterday it turned up again
from a heap of discarded 'paperasses,' and I think it
may as well be posted to you, to be read or not as you
please. You know that I do not want it to be returned
to me: but I do want you to send me a line concerning yourself, and your own health, which you somewhat
complained of in your last.

I have been away for a week to make my one visit:
which is to George Crabbe, my Poet's Grandson, a
Parson in Norfolk, and one of the most amiable,
intelligent, and agreeable of men. But my object in
going was less to see him (whom I catch a sight of
otherwise now and then)—not so much him, I say,

as his two Sisters, whom I also much regard, and whom I never see but when I look for them at his house. We had a very pleasant week together.

Some little while before this, I was meditating a much longer Journey, which was to have included Jersey! and yourself in it! and then a flight across to Brittany—with one single object in view; and that was—just to look at my dear old Sévigné's home near Vitré, and then—home again: just as when I had seen Sir Walter Scott's Abbotsford. I had been reading her through again; and felt a desire to realise what I read so much, and so delightfully, about; a desire I had often felt before, and which will, I suppose, never get further. You know by yourself that one becomes very slow to move so far at our time of Life. A note from old Spedding some days ago told me that Alfred, and his Son Hallam, were gone to Venice: so he is apparently not so superannuated as you and I. But then he has a Son who acts Courier for him. I could travel anywhere if quite at ease; but Steam Boats, Rails, Hotels, etc., all to be settled with, as well as to be endured, are now too much for me. I should have thought the season was rather far advanced for Venice, which, I believe, smells badly in Summer. Here in England we have not yet Heat to complain of: and Hay in the Field, and Mignonette in the Garden are better than stagnant Offal.

Now, write me a few lines to tell me you are better; and always believe me your ancient Friend.

EDWARD FITZGERALD

[WOODBRIDGE, *July* 24, 1880.]

MY DEAR LADY,

.｡.｡.One of my old Friends—and Flames—Mary Lynn (pretty name) who is of our age, and played with me when we both were Children—at that very same Aldeburgh—is gone over to those Mountains which you are so fond of: having the same passion for them as you have. I had asked her to meet me at that Aldeburgh—'Aldbro''—that we might ramble together along that beach where once we played; but she was gone.

If you should come to Lowestoft instead of Scarbro', we, if you please, will ramble together too. But I do not recommend the place—very ugly—on a dirty Dutch Sea—and I do not suppose you would care for any of my People; unless it were my little Niece Annie, who is a delightful Creature.

To Miss Anna Biddell.

Nov. 30, 1880.

One day I went into the Abbey at $3\frac{1}{2}$ p.m. while a beautiful anthem was beautifully sung, and then the prayers and collects, not less beautiful, well intoned on one single note by the Minister. And when I looked up and about me, I thought that Abbey a wonderful structure for Monkeys to have raised. The last night, Mesdames Kemble and Edwards had each of them company, so I went into my old Opera House in the Haymarket, where I remembered the very place where Pasta stood as Medea on the Stage, and Rubini singing his return to his Betrothed in the Puritani, and Taglioni floating everywhere about: and the several Boxes in which sat the several Ranks and Beauties of forty and fifty years ago: my Mother's Box on the third Tier, in which I often figured as a Specimen of both. The Audience all changed much for the worse, I thought: and Opera and Singers also; only one of them who could sing at all, and she sang very well indeed; Trebelli, her name. The opera by a Frenchman on the Wagner plan: excellent instrumentation, but not one new or melodious idea through the whole.

WOODBRIDGE: *Dec*. 6, [1880.]

MY DEAR LADY,

...Why will you take into your head that I could suppose you wanting in Hospitality, or any other sort of Generosity! That, at least, is not a Kemble failing. Why, I believe you would give me—and a dozen others—£1000 if you fancied one wanted it—even without being asked. The Law of Mede and Persian is that you *will* take up—a perverse notion—now and then. There! It's out.

As to the Tea—'pure and simple'—with Bread and Butter—it is the only meal I do care to join in :— and this is why I did not see Mowbray Donne, who has not his Dinner till an hour and a half after my last meal is done.

I should very gladly have 'crushed a Cup of Tea' with you that last Evening, coming prepared so to do. But you had Friends coming; and so (as Mrs. Edwards was in the same plight) I went to the Pit of my dear old Haymarket Opera:[1] remembering the very corner of the Stage where Pasta stood when Jason's People came to tell her of his new Marriage; and (with one hand in her Girdle—a movement (Mrs. Frere said) borrowed from Grassini) she interrupted them with her " Cessate—intesi ! "—also when Rubini, feathered hat in hand, began that " Ah te, oh Cara " —and Taglioni hovered over the Stage.   There was the old Omnibus Box too where D'Orsay flourished in ample white Waistcoat and Wristbands: and Lady Blessington's: and Lady Jersey's on the Pit tier: and my own Mother's, among the lesser Stars, on the third.   In place of all which I dimly saw a small Company of less distinction in all respects; and heard an Opera (*Carmen*) on the Wagner model : very beautiful Accompaniments to no Melody: and all very badly sung except by Trebelli, who, excellent. I ran out in the middle to the dear Little Haymarket opposite—where Vestris and Liston once were: and found the Theatre itself spoilt by being cut up into compartments which marred the beautiful Horse-shoe shape, once set off by the flowing pattern of Gold which used to run round the house.

Enough of these Old Man's fancies—But—Right for all that ! . . .

Poets to do some such service for their Predecessors.

I hope this long letter is tolerably legible : and I am in very truth

Sincerely yours

THE LAIRD OF LITTLEGRANGE.

To W. A. Wright.

[*March* 10, 1881.]

MY DEAR WRIGHT,

...I had asked Carlyle's Niece for the Bowl and an inch or two of the stem of such Clay pipes as I used to smoke with Carlyle under a little Pear tree — I think it was — in the little garden-plot behind his Chelsea house. She has sent me a handsome old Meerschaum, as you will see by the enclosed : for which, as I tell her, I am almost sorry, considering that he had many friends really much more worthy of it in many ways than myself : and that I have so short a time of my own to possess it. I ask her if she would like me to bequeathe it to any one ? If not, it will pass into the hands of my little Annie Niece, who will not throw it away—nor sell it !

I think I can see Carlyle, changed as he was from twenty-five years ago, hearing of Spedding's Accident and its Result. I believe that, unless he were as for the last three weeks of his Life he was, he would have had himself carried to St George's Hospital.

Mowbray Donne wrote me that Laurence had been

there four or five days ago, when Spedding said, that had the Cab done but a little more, it would have been a good Quietus. Socrates to the last.

20 *March*, [1881.]

MY DEAR LADY,

I have let the Full Moon pass because I thought you had written to me so lately, and so kindly, about our lost Spedding, that I would not call on you too soon again. Of him I will say nothing except that his Death has made me recall very many passages in his Life in which I was partly concerned. In particular, staying at his Cumberland Home along with Tennyson in the May of 1835. 'Voilà bien long temps de ça!' His Father and Mother were both alive — he, a wise man, who mounted his Cob after Breakfast, and was at his Farm till Dinner at two—then away again till Tea: after which he sat reading by a shaded lamp: saying very little, but always courteous, and quite content with any company his Son might bring to the house so long as they let him go his way: which indeed he would have gone whether they let him or no. But he had seen enough of Poets not to like them or their Trade: Shelley, for a time living among the Lakes: Coleridge at Southey's (whom perhaps he had a respect for—Southey, I mean), and Wordsworth, whom I do not think he valued. He was rather jealous of 'Jem,' who might have done available service in the world, he thought, giving himself up to such Dreamers ; and sitting up with Tennyson conning over the Morte d'Arthur, Lord of Burleigh, and other things which helped to make up the two Volumes of 1842. So I always associate that Arthur Idyll with Basanthwaite Lake, under Skiddaw. Mrs. Spedding was a sensible, motherly Lady, with whom I used to play Chess of a Night. And there was an old Friend of hers, Mrs. Bristow, who always reminded me of Miss La Creevy, if you know of such a Person in Nickleby.

At the end of May we went to lodge for a week at Windermere—where Wordsworth's new volume of Yarrow Revisited reached us. W. was then at his home : but Tennyson would not go to visit him : and of course I did not : nor even saw him. ᵥᵥ..

...Here is a dull and coldish Day after the fine ones we have had—which kept me out of doors as long as they lasted. Now one turns to the Fireside again. To-morrrow is Equinox Day ; when, if the Wind should return to North East, North East will it blow till June 21, as we all believe down here. My Eyes are better, I presume to say : but not what they were even before Christmas. Pray let me hear how you are, and believe me ever the same

E. F.G.

[*April*, 1881.]

My dear Mrs. Kemble,

Somewhat before my usual time, you see, but Easter comes, and I shall be glad to hear if you

keep it in London, or elsewhere. Elsewhere there
has been no inducement to go until To-day : when
the Wind, though yet East, has turned to the Southern
side of it : one can walk without any wrapper ; and
I dare to fancy we have turned the corner of Winter
at last. People talk of changed Seasons : only yesterday I was reading in my dear old Sévigné, how she
was with the Duke and Duchess of Chaulnes at their
Château of Chaulnes in Picardy all but two hundred
years ago ; that is in 1689 : and the green has not as
yet ventured to show its 'nez' nor a Nightingale to
sing. You see that I have returned to her as for
some Spring Music, at any rate. As for the Birds, I
have nothing but a Robin, who seems rather pleased
when I sit down on a Bench under an Ivied Pollard,
where I suppose he has a Nest, poor little Fellow.
But we have terrible Superstitions about him here ;
no less than that he always kills his Parents if he
can : my young Reader is quite determined on this
head : and there lately has been a Paper in some
Magazine to the same effect.

My dear old Spedding sent me back to old Wordsworth too, who sings (his best songs, I think) about
the Mountains and Lakes they were both associated
with : and with a quiet feeling he sings, that somehow comes home to me more now than ever it did
before. . . .

Well—I am expecting Aldis Wright here at Easter :
and a young London Clerk (this latter I did invite
for his short holiday, poor Fellow !) Wright is to
read me 'The Two Noble Kinsmen.'

And now I have written more than enough for yourself and me : whose Eyes may be the worse for it to-morrow. I still go about in Blue Glasses, and flinch from Lamp and Candle. Pray let me know about your own Eyes, and your own Self ; and believe me always sincerely yours

LITTLEGRANGE.

I really was relieved that you did not write to thank me for the poor flowers which I sent you. They were so poor that I thought you would feel bound so to do, and, when they were gone, repented. I have now some gay Hyacinths up, which make my patty-pan Beds like China Dishes.

[*April*, 1881.]

MY DEAR LADY :

...It has been what we call down here 'smurring' rather than raining, all day long : and I think that Flower and Herb already show their gratitude. My Blackbird (I think it is the same I have tried to keep alive during the Winter) seems also to have 'wetted his Whistle,' and what they call the 'Cuckoo's mate,' with a rather harsh scissor note, announces that his Partner may be on the wing to these Latitudes. You will hear of him at Mr. W. Shakespeare's, it may be. There must be Violets, white and blue, somewhere about where he lies, I think. They are generally found in a Churchyard, where also (the Hunters used to say) a Hare : for the same reason of comparative security, I suppose. . . .

May 8, [1881.]

MY DEAR MRS. KEMBLE:

...I am got back to my—Sévigné!—who somehow returns to me in Spring: fresh as the Flowers. These latter have done but badly this Spring, cut off or withered by the Cold: and now parched up by this blazing Sun and dry Wind. If you get my letter, pray answer it and tell me how you are: and ever believe me yours

LITTLEGRANGE.

To W. A. Wright.

WOODBRIDGE, *August* 20, 1881.

MY DEAR WRIGHT,

As you did not annotate to your Parne-Creighton slip [1] that it was to be returned to you, I have kept, and keep it, you see, till further orders. It is a touching old thing of the Past: your part of the work, as always, all that it should be.

I was at old Beccles during the last two or three days, when you were at Somerleyton—from Wednesday till Saturday of last week—at the old King's Head: whence I radiated to Geldestone and Lowestoft in the day-time; sitting with my dear old Crowfoot in the evenings. I had wanted to see over old Geldestone haunts, not seen these dozen years; as also some of those about old Beccles, which I love too for its quaint irregularity, grand Church Tower, and Market-place, on which I sat looking when my reading Eyes were tired. I went to your house: but all Blinds were down, so that I knew you were not within; and even the Garden gate padlocked, so that I could not ask about you. 'Voilà qui est fait' so far as Beccles is concerned. That is, for the present: for I shall feel myself drawn thither again, I think before this Autumn is gone.

[*Nov.* 1881.]

MY DEAR LADY:

...I am sorry you are gone again to Westminster, to which I cannot reconcile myself as to our old London. Even Bloomsbury recalls to me the pink May which used to be seen in those old Squares— sixty years ago. But 'enfin, voilà qui est fait.' You know where that comes from. I have not lately been in company with my old dear: Annie Thackeray's Book[1] is a pretty thing for Ladies in a Rail carriage; but my old Girl is scarce half herself in it. And there are many inaccuracies, I think. Mais enfin, voilà, etc. . . .

I have only just got my Garden laid up for the winter, and planted some trees in lieu of those which that last gale blew down. I hear that Kensington Gardens suffered greatly: how was it with your Green Park, on which you now look down from such a height, and, I suppose, through a London Fog?

Ever yours
LITTLE G.

[1] On Madame de Sévigné.

EDWARD FITZGERALD

To F. Tennyson.

Dec. 1881.

My dear old Frederic,

I must not let Christmas and the Old Year pass away without a loving word from me. You know that I have but little more to say: for I have seen and heard less all this year than any year before, I think: and have at present little new to report of my own personal condition.

Let me hear at least as much, and as well, of yourself.

I wrote to Alfred a month or so ago: and was answer'd (for a wonder) by Hallam—from Aldworth —telling me that all were pretty well—his Father 'walking and working as usual.' They (Hallam and he) had not long before been a trip to Stratford-on-Avon and Sherwood Forest: finding the latter such a piece of Old England as Washington Irving had described. I suppose they went before that October Gale half stript the Trees, even the Oaks, for which Sherwood is celebrated. Perhaps, however, the Gale did not rage there as hereabout it did: blowing down four of the best of my few trees. And another Gale about a month ago blew down paling, and even Wall, for me. You can tell me how it fared with you in Jersey, from over which the Wind came. . . .

I suppose that you in Jersey have had no Winter yet: for even here thrushes pipe a little, anemones make a pale show, and I can sit in my indoor clothing on a Bench without, so long as the Sun shines. I can read but little, and count of my Boy's coming at Night, to read Sir Walter Scott, or some Travel or Biography, that amuses him as well as me. We are now beginning The Fortunes of Nigel, which I had not expected to care for, and shall possibly weary of before it ends : but the outset is nothing less than *delightful* to me. I think that Miss Austen, George Eliot and Co. have not yet quite extinguished him, in his later lights.

Now, my dear old Friend, I will shut up Shop before Christmas. Ah! I sincerely wish you were here ; and I do remain what for so many years I have been,

Your affectionate

OLD FITZ.

[Feb. 1882.]

MY DEAR MRS. KEMBLE :

...I see my poor little Aconites—'New Year's Gifts' —still surviving in the Garden-plot before my window ; 'still surviving,' I say, because of their having been out for near a month agone. I believe that Messrs. Daffodil, Crocus and Snowdrop are putting in appearance above ground : but (old Coward) I have not put my own old Nose out of doors to look for them.

I read (Eyes permitting) the Correspondence between Goethe and Schiller (translated) from 1798 to 1806 —extremely interesting to me, though I do not understand—and generally skip—the more purely Æsthetic Part: which is the Part of Hamlet, I suppose. But, in other respects, two such men so freely discussing together their own, and each other's, works interest me greatly. At Night, we have The Fortunes of Nigel; a little of it—and not every night: for the reason that I do not wish to eat my Cake too soon. The last night but one I sent my Reader to see Macbeth played by a little 'Shakespearian' company at a Lecture Hall here. He brought me one new Reading—suggested, I doubt not, by himself, from a remembrance of Macbeth's tyrannical ways: 'Hang out our *Gallows* on the outward walls.' Nevertheless, the Boy took great Interest in the Play; and I like to encourage him in Shakespeare, rather than in the Negro Melodists.

Such a long Letter as I have written (and, I doubt, ill written) really calls for Apology from me, busy as you may be with those Proofs. But still believe me sincerely yours

Though Laird of LITTLEGRANGE.

To W. A. Wright.

Friday [24 *February* 1882].

MY DEAR WRIGHT,

I went to London this day week: saw my poor Donne (rather better than I had expected to find him—but all declining) three times: and came home —glad to come home !—on Monday. Mrs. Kemble,

Edwards (Keene at the latter Lady's) and my old Nursey friends, all I saw beside, in the human way, save Streetfarers, Cabmen, etc. The Shops seemed all stale to me: the only Exhibition I went to (Old Masters) ditto. So I suppose that I have lost my Appetite for all but dull Woodbridge Life. I have not lost my Cold—nor all its bronchial symptoms; but may do so—as I get a little older.

Tennyson was in London, I heard: but in some grand Locality of Eaton Square; so I did not venture down to him. But a day scarcely passes without my thinking of him, in one way or other.

Browning told Mrs. Kemble he knew there was 'a grotesque side' to his Society, etc., but he could not refuse the kind solicitations of his Friends, Furnivall and Co. Mrs. K. had been asked to join: but declined, because of her somewhat admiring him; nay, much admiring what he might have done. . . . . .

To F. Tennyson.

March 1882.

MY DEAR FREDERIC,

A fortnight ago I was in London for three days: mainly to see my dear old Schoolfellow W. Donne, declining in Body and Mind: glad to see me, I believe. Two visits I paid to Mrs. Kemble: who told me that Alfred was in Town—in, or about, Eaton Square, I think: but as she said not a word of Hallam's Engagement, I presume that it was not then settled, or, at any rate, not reported. For Mrs. K., though [she] does not see more of Alfred than a visit or two in the course of the year, lives among those who hear all about him.

I had meant to hear some one opera of Wagner then playing at *my* old Opera House : but my three nights came and went without my doing so. I dare say I should not have stay'd out half—but then I could never do more with the finest Oratorio—but I should have heard The Music of the Future—sure to interest one in its orchestral expression, and if no Melody, none previously expected by me.

How pretty of the severe old Contrapuntist Cherubini saying to some one who complained of Bellini's meagre accompaniments—'They are all and just what is wanted for his beautiful simple Airs.' So when another found fault with Rossini's descent from 𝄞 to the Major 𝄢 he said he only wished he himself could have hit on such an irregularity. (I am speaking of the 3rd and 4th lines of the Prayer in Moïse, but I quote from Memory.)

I have not yet quite lost my Cold, and you know how one used to hear that so it was with Old Age : and now we find it so. Now the Sun shows his honest face I get more abroad, and have been sitting out under his blessed rays this very day, which People tell me is quite indiscreet. But I do not find the breath from Heaven direct nearly so trying as through a Keyhole.

What do you think of The 'Browning Society,' of which here is a sample cut from the last Academy?

'BROWNING SOCIETY (*Friday*, *Feb.* 24).

'Peter Bayne, Esq., in the Chair. Mr. J. T. Nettleship read a paper on "Fifine at the Fair,"' etc.

Imagine a Man abetting all this! Mrs. Kemble says he does *not* abet, and admits there is a 'grotesque side to it.' But he supplied a Mr. Gosse with particulars of his early Life and Inspirations for an American Magazine—which I will send you if I can find it. Born at Camberwell. I always said it could not be far from Bow Bells. . . .

LITTLEGRANGE: WOODBRIDGE,
March 31, [1882.]

DEAR MRS. KEMBLE:—

It is not yet full Moon: —but it is my 74th Birthday: and you are the only one whom I write to on that great occasion. A good Lady near here told me she meant to pay me a visit of congratulation: and I begged her to stay at home, and neither say, nor write, anything about it. . .

There is already a flush of Green, not only on the hedges, but on some of the trees; all things for-warder, I think, by six weeks than last year. Here is a Day for entering on seventy-four! But I do think, notwithstanding, that I am not much the better for it. The Cold I had before Christmas, returns, or

lurks about me : and I cannot resolve on my usual
out-of-door liberty. Enough of that. I suppose that
I shall have some Company at Easter ; my poor
London Clerk, if he can find no more amusing place
to go to for his short Holyday ; probably Aldis
Wright, who always comes into these parts at these
Seasons—his ' Nazioné ' being Beccles. Perhaps
also a learned Nephew of mine—John De Soyres—
now Professor of some History at Queen's College,
London, may look in. . . .

[*August*, 1882.]

MY DEAR MRS. KEMBLE,

I have let the Full Moon go by, and very
well she looked, too—over the Sea by which I am
now staying. Not at Lowestoft : but at the old
extinguished Borough of Aldeburgh, to which—as to
other ' premiers Amours,' I revert—where more than
sixty years ago I first saw, and first felt, the Sea—
where I have lodged in half the houses since ; and
where I have a sort of traditional acquaintance with
half the population. ' Clare Cottage ' is where I write
from ; two little rooms—enough for me—a poor civil
Woman pleased to have me in them—oh, yes,—and a
little spare Bedroom in which I stow a poor Clerk,
with his Legs out of the window from his bed—
like a Heron's from his nest—but rather more
horizontally. We dash about in Boats whether Sail
or Oar—to which latter I leave him for his own good
Exercise. Poor fellow, he would have liked to tug at

that, or rough-ride a horse, from Boyhood : but must be made Clerk in a London Lawyer's Office : and so I am glad to get him down for a Holyday when he can get one, poor Fellow!

The Carlyle ' Reminiscences ' had long indisposed me from taking up the Biography. But when I began, and as I went on with that, I found it one of the most interesting of Books : and the result is that I not only admire and respect Carlyle more than ever I did : but even love him, which I never thought of before. For he loved his Family, as well as for so long helped to maintain them out of very slender earnings of his own ; and, so far as these two Volumes show me, he loved his Wife also, while he put her to the work which he had been used to see his own Mother and Sisters fulfil, and which was suitable to the way of Life which he had been used to. His in-difference to her sufferings seems to me rather because of Blindness than Neglect; and I think his Biographer has been even a little too hard upon him on the score of Selfish disregard of her.

ALDEBURGH : *Sept.* 1, [1882.]

My dear Mrs. Kemble :

Still by the Sea—from which I saw *The Harvest Moon* rise for her three nights' Fullness. And to-day is so wet that I shall try and pay you my plenilunal due—not much to your satisfaction ; for the Wet really gets into one's Brain and Spirits, and I have as little to write of as ever any Full Moon ever

brought me. And yet, if I accomplish my letter, and
'take it to the Barber's,' where I sadly want to go,
and, after being wrought on by him, post my letter—
why, you will, by your Laws, be obliged to answer it.
Perhaps you may have a little to tell me of yourself
in requital for the very little you have to hear of me.

I have made a new Acquaintance here. Professor
Fawcett (Postmaster General, I am told) married a
Daughter of one Newson Garrett of this Place, who
is also Father of your Doctor Anderson. Well, the
Professor (who was utterly blinded by the Discharge
of his Father's Gun some twenty or twenty-five years
ago) came to this Lodging to call on Aldis Wright;
and, when Wright was gone, called on me, and also
came and smoked a Pipe one night here. A
thoroughly unaffected, unpretending, man ; so modest
indeed that I was ashamed afterwards to think how
I had harangued him all the Evening, instead of
getting him to instruct me. But I would not ask
him about his Parliamentary Shop : and I should
not have understood his Political Economy : and I
believe he was very glad to be talked to instead,
about some of those he knew, and some whom I had
known. And, as we were both in Crabbe's Borough,
we talked of him : the Professor, who had never read
a word, I believe, about him, or of him, was pleased
to hear a little ; and I advised him to buy the Life
written by Crabbe's Son ; and I would give him my
Abstract of the Tales of the Hall, by way of giving
him a taste of the Poet's self.

Yes ; you must read Froude's Carlyle above all

things, and tell me if you do not feel as I do about it. Professor Norton persists in it that I am proof against Froude's invidious insinuations simply because of my having previously known Carlyle. But how is it that I did not know that Carlyle was so good, grand, and even loveable, till I read the Letters which Froude now edits? I regret that I did not know what the Book tells us while Carlyle was alive; that I might have loved him as well as admired him. But Carlyle never spoke of himself in that way: I never heard him advert to his Works and his Fame, except one day he happened to mention 'About the time when Men began to talk of me.'. . .

To F. Tennyson.

September 9/82.

MY DEAR FREDERIC,

Pray let me hear of you. I have not dated this letter from where I am, and have been for the last six weeks—viz. Aldeburgh—Crabbe's old 'Borough,' by the Sea—because I am to be home at Woodbridge in two days. Crabbe's old Borough; and an Ancient Man (aged ninety-six) who served on board the Unity Sloop which took him to London when he went to seek his Fortune there: and did eventually find it, in Burke. I have known the Place from a Child: well remembering my first terror at being ruthlessly ducked into the Wave that came like a devouring Monster under the awning of the Bathing Machine

—a Machine whose Inside I hate to this Day. The Borough has but little to recommend it, and is so far more agreeable to Mark Tapley as it attracts but few, and those very quiet, Visitors. Yesterday a Man came up to me whom I had not seen for fifty years : I did not recognise him when he told me his name. I walk about, and sit about, and get about in Boats, and (having no Reader here) get to bed (after a Pipe) sometimes before Ten o'clock. Bronchitis occasionally reminds me that I am not forgotten by him ; but, on the contrary, that he will most probably take up his Quarters—and most probably, for good—when winter sets in. So I rather dread returning to the home where I had so many months of him this year : but it would be all the same if I remained here, or went anywhere, but to those far-away places whither I would scarce be at the trouble of going. *Cui bono ?* I am better off than many—if not most—of my contemporaries ; and there is not much [worth] living for after seventy-four.

I have read but very little lately, partly because the last Box from Mudie's did not contain much to interest me ; and partly because the glare of Sea and Shingle, unrelieved by a stripe of Green, indisposes my Eyes to Book-work.

Well now, in spite of this, I have written you a longish letter such as it is ; and you must send me one to read, all about yourself, if you please.

MY DEAR MRS. KEMBLE :

I suppose that you are returned from the
Loire by this time; but as I am not sure that you
have returned to the 'Hotel des Deux Mondes,'
whence you dated your last, I make bold once more
to trouble Coutts with adding your Address to my
Letter. I think I shall have it from yourself not long
after. I shall like to hear a word about my old
France, dear to me from childish associations; and
in particular of the Loire endeared to me by Sévigné
—for I never saw the glimmer of its Waters myself.
If you were in England I should send you an account
of a tour there, written by a Lady in 1833—written
in the good old way of Ladies' writing, without any
of the smartness, and not too much of the 'graphic'
of later times. Did you look at Les Rochers, which,
I have read, is not to be looked *into* by the present
owner?

Now for my 'Story, God bless you,' etc., you may
guess where none is to be told. Only, my old Housekeeper here has been bedded for this last month, an
illness which has caused her great pain, and at one
time seemed about to make an End of her. So it may
do still : but for the last few days she has suffered less
pain, and so we—hope. This has caused much
trouble in my little household, as you may imagine—
as well on our own account, as on hers.

Mowbray Donne wrote me that his Edith had been
seriously—I know not if dangerously—ill; and he
himself much out of sorts, having never yet (he says,

and I believe) recovered from his Father's death. Blanche, for the present, is quartered at Friends' and Kinsfolk's houses.

Aldis Wright has sent me a Photograph, copied from Mrs. Cameron's original, of James Spedding— so fine that I know not whether I feel more pleasure or pain in looking at it. When you return to England, you shall see it somehow.

You may have seen—but more probably have not seen—how Mr. Irving and Co. have brought out ' Much Ado' with all *éclat*.

It seems to me (but I believe it seems so every year) that our trees keep their leaves very long; I suppose because of no severe frosts or winds up to this time. And my garden still shows some Geranium, Salvia, Nasturtium, Great Convolvulus, and that grand African Marigold whose Colour is so comfortable to us Spanish-like Paddies. I have also a dear Oleander which even now has a score of blossoms on it, and touches the top of my little Greenhouse—having been sent me when 'haut comme ça,' as Marquis Somebody used to say in the days of Louis XIV. Don't you love the Oleander? So clean in its leaves and stem, as so beautiful in its flower; loving to stand in water, which it drinks up so fast. I rather worship mine.

[*Nov.*, 1882.]

MY DEAR MRS. KEMBLE:
...I have been again—twice or thrice—to Aldeburgh, when my contemporary old Beauty Mary Lynn was

staying there; and pleasant Evenings enough we had, talking of other days, and she reading to me some of her Mudie Books, finishing with a nice little Supper, and some hot grog (for me) which I carried back to the fire, and *set on the carpet.* She read me (for one thing) 'Marjorie Fleming' from a Volume of Dr. Brown's Papers —read it as well as she could for laughing—' idiotically,' she said—but all the better to my mind. She had been very dismal all day, she said. Pray get some one to read you 'Marjorie'— which I say, because (as I found) it agrees with one best in that way. If only for dear Sir Walter's sake, who doated on the Child; and would not let his Twelfth Night be celebrated till she came through the Snow in a Sedan Chair, where (once in the warm Hall) he called all his Company down to see her nestling before he carried her upstairs in his arms. A very pretty picture. My old Mary said that Mr. Anstey's 'Vice Versa' made her and a friend, to whom she read it, laugh idiotically too: but I could not laugh over it alone, very clever as it is. And here is enough of me and Mary.

To C. E. Norton.

WOODBRIDGE. *March* 7/83.

MY DEAR NORTON,

One day you must write, and tell me how you and yours have fared through this winter. It has been a very mild, even, a warm, one over here; and I for my part have not yet had much to complain of in point of health thus far; no, not even though winter has come at last in Snow and Storm for the last three days. I do not know if we are yet come to the worst, so terrible a Gale has been predicted, I am told, for the middle of March. Yesterday morning I distinctly heard the sea moaning some dozen miles away; and to-day, why, the enclosed little scrap,[1] enclosed to me, will tell you what it was about, on my very old Crabbe's shore. It (the Sea) will assuredly cut off his old Borough from the Slaughden River-quay where he went to work, and whence he sailed in the 'Unity' Smack (one of whose Crew is still alive) on his first adventure to London. But all this can but little interest you, considering that we in England (except some few in this Eastern corner of it) scarce know more of Crabbe and his where-about than by name.

To C. E. Norton.

WOODBRIDGE. *May* 12/83.

MY DEAR NORTON,

Your Emerson-Carlyle of course interested me very much, as I believe a large public also. I had most to learn of Emerson, and that all good: but Carlyle came out in somewhat of a new light to me also. Now we have him in his Jane's letters, as we

[1] A newspaper cutting: 'ALDEBURGH. THE STORM. On Tuesday evening the tide ran over the Promenade, in many places the river and sea meeting. The cattle are all sent inland, and all the houses at Slaughden are evacuated.'

had seen something of him before in the Reminiscences : but a yet more tragic Story ; so tragic that I know not if it ought not to have been withheld from the Public : assuredly, it seems to me, ought to have been but half of the whole that now is. But I do not the less recognize Carlyle for more admirable than before—if for no other reason than his thus furnishing the world with weapons against himself which the World in general is glad to turn against him. . . .

And, by way of finishing what I have to say on Carlyle for the present, I will tell you that I had to go up to our huge, hideous, London a week ago, on disagreeable business; which Business, however, I got over in time for me to run to Chelsea before I returned home at Evening. I wanted to see the Statue on the Chelsea Embankment which I had not yet seen : and the old No. 5 of Cheyne Row, which I had not seen for five and twenty years. The Statue I thought very good, though looking somewhat small and ill set-off by its dingy surroundings. And No. 5 (now 24), which had cost her so much of her Life, one may say, to make habitable for him, now all neglected, unswept, ungarnished, uninhabited

‘TO LET’   I cannot get it out of my head, the tarnished Scene of the Tragedy (one must call it) there enacted.

Well, I was glad to get away from it, and the London of which it was a small part, and get down here to my own dull home, and by no means sorry not to be a Genius at such a Cost. ' Parlons d'autres choses.'. . . .

[*May*, 1883.]

MY DEAR LADY;

...At last some feeling of Spring—a month before Midsummer. And next week I am expecting my grave Friend Charles Keene, of Punch, to come here for a week—bringing with him his Bagpipes, and an ancient Viol, and a Book of Strathspeys and Madrigals; and our Archdeacon will come to meet him, and to talk over ancient Music and Books : and we shall all three drive out past the green hedges, and heaths with their furze in blossom—and I wish—yes, I do— that you were of the Party.

I love all Southey, and all that he does; and love that Correspondence of his with Caroline Bowles. We (Boy and I) have been reading an account of Zetland, which makes me thirst for 'The Pirate' again—tiresome, I know, more than half of it—but what a Vision it leaves behind !

Now, Madam, you cannot pretend that you have to jump at my meaning through my MS. I am sure it is legible enough, and that I am ever yours

E. F.G.

To S. Laurence.

WOODBRIDGE. *Tuesday,*
[*June* 12, 1883].

MY DEAR LAURENCE,

It is very kind of you to remember one who does so little to remind you of himself. Your drawing of Allen always seemed to me excellent, for which reason it was that I thought his Wife should have it, as being the Record of her husband in his younger days. So of the portrait of Tennyson which I gave his Wife. Not that I did not value them myself, but because I did value them, as the most agreeable Portraits I knew of the two men; and, for that very reason, presented them to those whom they were naturally dearer to than even to myself. I have never liked any Portrait of Tennyson since he grew a Beard; Allen, I suppose, has kept out of that.

If I do not write, it is because I have absolutely nothing to tell you that you have not known for the last twenty years. Here I live still, reading, and being read to, part of my time; walking abroad three or four times a day, or night, in spite of wakening a Bronchitis, which has lodged like the household 'Brownie' within; pottering about my Garden (as I have just been doing) and snipping off dead Roses like Miss Tox; and now and then a visit to the neighbouring Seaside, and a splash to Sea in one of the Boats. I never see a new Picture, nor hear a note of Music except when I drum out some old Tune in Winter on an Organ, which might almost be carried about the Streets with a handle to turn, and a Monkey on the top of it. So I go on, living a life far too comfortable as compared with that of better, and wiser men : but ever expecting a reverse in health such as my seventy-five years are subject to. . . .To-morrow I am going (for my one annual Visit) to G. Crabbe's, where I am to meet his Sisters, and talk over old Bredfield Vicarage days. Two of my eight Nieces are now with me here in my house, for a two months' visit, I suppose and hope. And I think this is all I have to tell you of

Yours ever sincerely
E. F.G.

_____